I am twenty people!

A third anthology from The Poetry School 2004–2006

Edited by
Mimi Khalvati & Stephen Knight

ENITHARMON PRESS

First published in 2007
by Enitharmon Press
26B Caversham Road
London NW5 2DU

www.enitharmon.co.uk

Distributed in the UK by
Central Books
99 Wallis Road
London E9 5LN

Distributed in the USA and Canada
by Dufour Editions Inc.
PO Box 7, Chester Springs
PA 19425, USA

ISBN: 978-1-904634-36-2

Enitharmon Press gratefully acknowledges the financial support of
Arts Council England, London.

British Library Cataloguing-in-Publication Data.
A catalogue record for this book is available
from the British Library.

Designed by Libanus Press
and printed in England by
Antony Rowe Ltd

CONTENTS

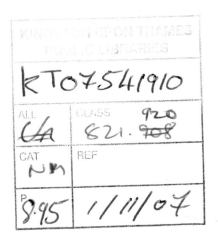

INTRODUCTION

This year marks the tenth anniversary of The Poetry School. *I am twenty people!* celebrates this occasion, and is the third anthology of an ongoing series from Enitharmon Press that aims to bring the work of new poets to a wider readership.

Our first anthology, *Tying the Song*, presented substantial selections from eleven poets while *Entering the Tapestry* introduced the poetry of thirty of our participants. Here, we showcase something between the two – poems from twenty people that happily confirm the wealth of talent we as editors were able to draw from. Not only were there many potential contributors for us to consider but their work also offered the variety of approach characteristic of the School. Much of the writing in *I am twenty people!* sidesteps the conventions of contemporary verse in favour of an adventurousness and independence of spirit we hope readers will enjoy. It seems that the poets themselves, perhaps impatient with the mainstream, have looked more widely, both geographically and historically, for their inspiration.

Drawing from recommendations made by tutors of The Poetry School, we invited submissions from a number of participants, many of whom we would have liked to represent, given more space. At the time of acceptance, none of the poets included in *I am twenty people!* had published a full-length volume, although some now have books forthcoming. The majority of contributors to our first anthology went on to publish collections. Contributors to both our previous anthologies number among their successes the Costa Book Award, a shortlisting for the T. S. Eliot Prize, the Forward Prize for Best First Collection, the Forward Prize for Best Poem, the Geoffrey Faber Memorial Prize, the Jerwood/Aldeburgh Prize for Best First Collection, New Writing Ventures Awards, and

Poetry Book Society Recommendations. We look forward to similar achievements for our present contributors.

The Poetry School believes in the reading and writing of poetry as a lifelong engagement, and we especially value those participants whose work continues to evolve and surprise. Three such poets, who were included in our second anthology, reappear here. All twenty of our poets have demonstrated serious commitment over the months and years they have attended The Poetry School, and have already achieved a fine range of ambitious work. We are confident that, given such dedication and talent, they will thrive in the years ahead.

MIMI KHALVATI
STEPHEN KNIGHT

'I am twenty people!'

from the diaries of Virginia Woolf,
quoted by Linda Black in
'At the Little Deal Table Under the Glare of the Lamp' (page 17)

Alice Allen

STUFF

If the body is to adorn the soul
how should it dress her? In lengths

of taffeta and silk powdered with opals
or bound into a cabinet of steel?

Does it matter if the soul dislocates
and glides unfettered, unreservedly

into the glisten and slick of the body,
a bauble pressing its weight in sequinned water?

The selvedge of the skin has its own softness
durable as sailcloth and more tender –

let the body if it finds her
dress the soul with this.

AMBUSH

What darkness is, coming in low
over the island; does it rest or wait?

I'm walking home and something in me
lingers as I choose the right lane

or is it only pausing for effect,
that the night should know me

to be slow and true to its momentum?
So when I, stumbling, lose my way

night will steer me from the finite
edges of the earth, where the sea

is slowly shifting in suspense
and the wind, before it turns, falters.

WE WOULD

She read the sky like an atlas
staring at the tracks between clouds,
her plait a moving spine of yellow corn.
Sometimes we'd stop and rest in tall grass
until rain ceased in the forest up ahead.
If we continued, she said, we'd drown
in thunder clouds. Mostly though we'd walk
the fields and hills, the scrawny coast,
her leading with starlings on her mind
and when we cried she'd turn,
her clear eyes looking as on dead things.
At night we'd find a mountain, cradle in its bones.

It was an age before I understood
there was no forest deluge up ahead,
no banks of cloud-dark thunder, only
sponge moss on the forest floor and everywhere
the ground alive with berries.

THE SEA'S LOAN TO THE CITY

When I woke this morning
  everything smelt good

as if the sea had come up slowly
  into London while we slept

softening the edges of the streets
  rubbing the buildings smooth

as if the sea isn't always with us
  while we don't look

shell chains locked inside
  the stone of our offices

sea lilies in the bricks of our homes.
  We have always breathed salt air

walking to work, crowds of us
  picking our way across oyster beds

to buildings where the tide has made
  white bracelets in the glass

and what is glass anyway
  if not the dream of sand?

Linda Black

AT THE LITTLE DEAL TABLE UNDER THE GLARE OF THE LAMP

(from the diaries of Virginia Woolf)

My feeling is half moonshine. I am trying to tell
whatever self it is cast shade upon me. An odd thing

the human mind, infinitely shying at shadows,
a little strip of pavement over an abyss. Here I sit.

Like a lantern in the middle of a field
my light goes up in darkness. I think too much

of whys and wherefores, can't settle
as I should. I am twenty people! I thought

I was becoming more myself. Here I am
chained to my rock, one touch of red

in the cheek, the machinery
a little cumbrous, a cloud in my head. I should

notice everything, the phrase for it coming
the moment after. These mists of spirit

have other causes; the shut up house;
dust sheets on the chairs, the least interesting of rooms,

the compromise, like little sips,
thin as a March glaze on a pool. I took a vow

I'd say what I thought, think myself
infallible, and so I write nonsense

that life mayn't be wasted. The windows
fidget at their fastenings. I feel now and then

a tug to vision, the little owl calling.
Yesterday the river burst its banks. My mind

works in idleness – I am stuffed with ideas!
– feel I can use up everything

I have ever thought. The soul swims
from one lighted room to another.

Last night I looked at the meadow – trees
flinging about, such a weight of leaves

every brandish seemed the end. I do not
love my kind – I let them break on me

like dirty raindrops, dry little shapes
floating past, second selves, obscure and odd.

Never mind. Arrange what pieces come your way, live
entirely in it and come to the surface

obscurely. I can float everything off now,
a crowd, a weight, a confusion in the mind, a sense

of my own strangeness; those mountain clouds,
a small stone, the fall of a flower. (She too feels wonder.)

Here's my interesting thing, and no quiet
solid table on which to put it.

(As if it upped and wandered) its seat dipped and splintered. *And the sun shall not heal*... O to sit on an imaginary (but one – a corner of – is known to me, is *almost* a reality ... I think of porches, a porch, *the porch*, a frosted glass enclosure, *encasement*, through which for some time I'd no choice but to pass) verandah, swinging my legs. Each chair I own is more or less uncomfortable; each dictates to me my thoughts.

Is she reaching out or turning away? Younger she is than I am now... *younger than springtime... something... than laughter...* I am dressed in white kid boots – I assume it was her tied the laces. What is 'kid' – is it like veal, pale with white blood, starved of light? And only part of her. Was it necessary, each step across the verandah; a right of passage, feet off ground, a small soul slightly elevated? And above that and above that ... up one staircase and then another ... towards the eves ... attic ... gabled roof... higher... higher. The harder to be rooted. And then came the bolder shoe, the longed-for height, toes forced into shoes with heels that spike. The further from. The out of reach.

But I've got there too soon. Shall I go back? Add a scene in which a mother is a mother and a daughter is good enough? *Or one where a father* (*Lindy! Sandy! Late for school!*) calls the wicked uncle to stop them fight, *or* where a powerless father puts an arm around a weeping daughter, *or* where the daughter sits on the stairs banging her head against the wall?

(You may think she was a mother of real fresh and blood, that the child with the finger in her mouth – what does it mean, that she placed her finger so, standing as she was on the veranda looking out over the balustrade down to whoever looked up at her? – was me. Is it insignificant that I think I recognise, through the veneer, through the leaded lights, through the reflection of an arch and a spindly tree, the swirled pattern on the curtains, of no

consequence the gap between rail and strut? Stave, lintel, pillar –
pane, paling, newel-post – each piece of timber, each endangered
brick, each portion of her, each cell, petrified.)

Verandah gives way to porch. By this time we don't talk or remem-
ber how or ever having done so. Each day has its routine: how to
sit, how not to, how to place a knife and fork when food is done,
how precisely to fold a shirt. Do you still have that picture of me –
the one 'not how you wanted me to be?' I have it too. Such a neat
cursive script, such well-formed letters – you could have been a
teacher. You must have had some friends.

MY FATHER

(1)

My father had six fingers, a hooked nose and one eye. My father had a hinged jaw and no teeth, a dewdrop and a pack of Woodbines. My father had a gold signet ring, swollen knuckles and his hands were claws. My father wore braces and shat in a bucket under the stairs. My father sat on a low stool lighting the boiler for hours. He sat on a high stool eating bananas and bread. My father had a mother but I did not know her. My father had a father but I did not know him. My father had a grey paisley scarf. My father made tea for my mother. But I did not know her. My father took me to the playground in Potternewton Park. This was before he had an iron leg. I spun round and round. My mother milked my father. My father opened the door to 'uncle' Charlie. My father nodded and shuffled. My mother's stepmother liked my father. She told me this in a car outside Chislehurst caves. She said it was a bad match. My mother told me 'I want never gets'. If he were here I think he would be standing, staring at nothing. I think he would be leaning backwards. I think he would look like he might fall over. My father had hollow legs.

(2)

Here is Sadie in a home, back from the dead. (No more holidays in Blackpool for the partially sighted.) Sadie with the big hair. Little-old-lady Sadie who remembered everyone's birthdays till she couldn't see to write, telling me again; 'Your daddy, ooh he was a lovely fella!' My daddy 'The Ginger Beer Man', delivering the lemonade on a Thursday in his horse and cart, coming back on the Sunday for his tuppence and a cup of tea. 'Ours-was-the-last-house'-Sadie. Anne comes every day to dress Sadie. Anne is sick and miserable. Mother and daughter don't get on. Anne's husband was weasly Maurice, executor of my father's will. (In this way he procured my mother's cocktail cabinet, Venetian glass, place mats, nest of tables and all her money.) My grandfather was a Maurice but called Mon. My brother-in-law is a Morris. Morris's mother was a Doris like my mother Doris. Morris and my sister (known by her second name) were given an old framed ad of a Morris Minor inscribed 'You'll be glad you married a Morris'.

(3)

My father is as motionless as one who is asleep and in the state of paralysis. My father is inert, as if he could be lifted in one piece and would not bend. My father is swaddled in a cocoon or wrapped in bandages. As if he has lain long in his nest. It has taken some time to notice his stillness. To see he is there. From sunset to sunset he has lain in his wraps, unable – as I now see – to withstand the journey. We must call a physician – of *his* race, *his* people. Have we been callous? My father requests a comb, which I do not have and all my venturing will not provide. For a moment he has risen, is propped upright. I admire the cloth of his tailored suit. I love my father, this little man, shrivelled to the smallest of beings.

SEVEN LAMPS

(after Ruskin)

Look abroad into the landscape
so bent and fragmentary: the flowing river,
its pebbled bed, out of the kneaded fields,
concretions of lime and clay loosely struck,
small habitations alike without difference, built
in the hope of leaving, lived in the hope
of forgetting, vanquished
in the hanging thickets of hillsides.
Ribands occur frequently in arabesques, flitting
hither and thither among the fixed forms,
apologetic, drifting into what they will,
no beginning nor end; no strength, no skeleton,
no make, no will of their own, only
flutter. Let the flowers come loose . . .

Long low lines rise, soon to be lifted
and wildly broken. Far-reaching ridges
rend their rude and changeful ways,
those ever-springing flowers, conquerors
of forgetfulness, more precious in memories
than in the renewing. The pavement rises
and falls, arches nod westward and sink, not one
of like height. These inclinations:
the accidental leaning, the curious incidence
of distortion – differences
in which they are lightly engaged,
exquisite delicacies of change tallied
to a hair's breadth – have grace
about them, a sensation in every inch.

The goodly street: many a pretty beading
and graceful bracket, the warm sleep of sunshine
upon it. Count its stones, set watches about it,
where it loosens bind it with iron, stay it with timber
tenderly. When the pitcher is rested, the breath
drawn deeply, what pause so sweet? In the declivity
of a hill, between the heights of stories, serenity
holds out its strong arm. But if to stone be added
intervals, arched and trefoiled, hangings of
purple and scarlet, taches of brass, sockets
of silver, twisted with tracery and starry light, charged
with wild fancy, I would fain introduce
a narrow door, a footworn sill, a hearth
of mica slate, a steel grate, a polished fender.

Rests and monotones settle at first
contentedly in the recess of a rose window.
Under the dark quietness, blunt-edged rosettes
neither bend nor grow. This interval – an arboresence,
a candied conglomorate through which we pass –
not that it is indolence or the feebleness
of childhood breaks away the bark
in noble rents. A life of custom and accident,
losing sight, animates, puts gestures
in clouds, voices into rock. A double creature,
feigned or unfeigned, speaks
what we do not mean, like the flow
of a lava stream, languid, settling,
crusted over with idle matter.

In the discontented present a certain deception,
the root unseen, spreads like a winding sheet.
Irregular stems of ivy run up hollows; a falling tendril,
the creeping thing. The very quietness of nature
restless against a dead wall. In the chasms and rents
of rocks, the wind has no power, ridge rising
over ridge in absolute bluntness. Cut
and crush what you will. More has been gleaned
out of desolation. At the meeting of the dark streets,
the spire with its pinnacles, winged griffins stirring
within the tympanum; in gloomy rows, disquieted walls,
shells of splintered wood, foundationless,
tottering. A desecrated landscape – walk
in sorrow, rend it lightly and pour out its ashes.

I once thought that which I could not love
diminished more than it increased.
The snow, the vapour and the stormy wind,
cold interiors of cathedrals bordered
by the impure in all the meanest
and most familiar forms – I could not bear
one drifting shower! Details,
even to the cracks in stones, rise,
strange and impatient, chrystallised
as with hoar frost. Memoranda
thrown together – I cannot answer
for accuracy. There is something
to be grateful for. Even weeds are useful
that grow on a bank of sand.

The hours of life, as if measured
by the angel's rod, let them be gathered
well together in woods and thickets,
in plains, cliffs and waters;
the setting forth of magnitude beheld
with never ceasing delight; infinity of fair form
– fairest in the quiet lake, the surface
wide, bold and unbroken, light
blossoming upon it. A great entail.
So again it sails! The face of a wall is
as nothing – is infinite! – its edge
against the sky like a horizon, the eye drawn
to its terminal lines. Time and storm
set their wild signatures.

Jemma Borg

THE PIECES WE NEED

We could say it had travelled along the waves
from one jigsaw end of the Pacific

to another and seen clouds lit up like lanterns
and schools of fish passing like fronts of weather,

sharks skimming the water's turquoise skin and islands,
far off, their rising houses of coral

made green with light. We could say: all this, to arrive
here and finally be still, the cushion

of depth giving way to this weight of landing.
And we could say that somewhere this story is true

or that pieces are, pieces we needed
to gather to account for this quiet jetsam

on its beach, its necessary puzzle:
the rubbish that lightened a ship. But the horizon

is hazy and can't be reached and, so too,
behind the shoreline, palms are growing in sand

which itself gives way to earth, to tarmac
and the long drive to the beach.

THE SCULPTURE

Since we've moved house, I've discovered
many things floating around us, organised
politely into circular layers

as a mandala is, linking our realm
of suffering and the mundane with its heaven.
Right above our heads, a TV's aura

agitates the wall with an indistinct drama.
Then, like guardians against dissolution,
there are fabrics and quilts in layers

of silks and matts and all the off-colours:
Egyptian beige, paisley and Flocket mint.
Then come the household goods, still sleeping in

their boxes and dirty with newspaper print,
the Xs of chromosomes pulling apart
like goodbye kisses and a frog transforming

into a man in twelve stages. Two lights
descend from the ceiling like white plastic eggs
and an ammonite reflects its secretive coil

in a mirror by the bedroom door. On our table,
which seats 2 to 4, there's a Thai wooden dragon,
a lamp with no bulb and a dish of plums

with their two halves of unripened twins.
In photos, I lean against you, the place
where we meet, side by side, limb to limb

very dark, but for now our frames display
only the blankness of cardboard and wait
for that picture of a sculpture I cut

from a magazine. Standing on a white base,
raised by a black stem, it looks like two sponges
budding off one another, while behind

a community of lights is always switched on:
a life made together already settled
into itself. I really must work harder

to mine our confinement. So, while you seem
to have speed around you, I have the near-
emptiness of shelves, as though even here

I have no past, just this one vase stretched
out into a tiny mouth. A composite face
is floating between us like dust in the sun

and despite your half and mine twisting round
each other like the caduceus' snakes,
it looks like neither of us. You're the solid

ground but I am more like circuitry
and though beauty is conferred by symmetry,
it's claimed, this is a union of both sorrow

and joy, a face refusing to reconcile
if either was lost. On the edges of us,
like translucent socks on a line, the skins

of snakes align themselves: multicoloured,
delicate and exhausted. How silences
have been multiplying, after, over

and among themselves, contained in each other
like Russian dolls, right down to this foetus
asleep in its perfect, untouchable form.

Right where our mouths should be, I've discovered
this sculpture, our solitary urchin,
opening its eyes like a ripe pomegranate.

It's been learning the sounds of our join.
What beautiful risks are lost from each other,
it whispers, our little growing sunshine,

both banal and sublime, eating the power
of opposition and throwing out
its own strange light. Thus, from the fog: this fire.

SOUL SENDS A LETTER AT LAST

Ah, you should see the light in Alexandria,
above the harbour, in the hour before noon.
I arrived here on Wednesday by train from Cairo,
the seats very generous in first class.

For a while, I was unsure of who I was
– the heat can be disconcerting – but I was glad
to be carrying a blanket, the air conditioning
rather chill after the desert, and even a dirty sea

would have been welcome, although that was
not what I found. Everything in the Sahara
had been one colour: the camels, the giant bricks
of the pyramids. It's only the sky that orientates you.

The ascent into the belly of the great Cheops,
to the small space they called 'tomb'
but where no king's swaddled body
was ever found, was as disconcerting:

was I travelling to the stars or burrowing
into the earth? I know your ear has been listening
for this letter, for its solemn little rectangle.
I'm sorry it's felt very silent, but so it is

we become mothers to each observed detail
of our separation and it's only at night
we miss one another, my dear. In the day,
I must confess, I barely remember your name.

DO I STILL THINK OF YOU?

after Gerard Manley Hopkins

I

I do still think of you but the feeling is lean.
    The world cannot gather its grandeur
or share things with us, and we cannot feel
    our bare being nor the rod of nature
on our bent backs. We do not rate spring;
    nor have we ever been so bleary-eyed.
We say: it is last, it is out, it is over. Sometimes
    we are sure our explanations are enough

to scratch the questions, but we are spent
    on the brink of emotion. Generations of sentences
brood and toil their difficult trade, your ghost
    holy and foolish, walking its silent thoughts
through the walls and into the nights.
    Now the world's feet, and ours, are shod.

II

My feet still think they are ears to the ground,
    shod with shining foil-wings for walking
with the bright-fantastic to the charged
    soil in the east. It's as though they can hear light
gathering fine and careful next to me. The world
    is seared in freshness; pearls of night ooze like oil
before the dawn, everything that was brown, pruned
    as in a sketch, becoming *almost* and then actually

becoming, like love bent and shaking warm
    from all the stuck corners, creating a day
which wears its grandeur without a man's
    crushed voice. This is not bare work, but a rod
of will and a plan, and it is the sun
    now setting out and out, collecting itself, westward.

AS FLAMINGOS AT THE WATER'S EDGE

dip their heads, so have I looked down
in surprise. It's as though glass has been falling
from my eyes, gathering at my feet and I've stepped on
the pieces of broken window, the shattered kryptonite,
the pins of jewellers' quartz on which gold chains
drape themselves like idle iguanas. It must be that tears
eventually freeze into fossils, harden like caramelised sugar,
scatter themselves as a glacier's debris, until I can't bear
to walk outside barefoot. You'd think I'd find myself
in a salt desert as white as coconut ice.
You'd expect the cataract of the Salar de Uyuni
against the sky, sun-encrusted with the hidden jewels of the sea
and the bacteria doing their complex, different chemistries
in an otherwise barren bowl. But instead I seem
to be in the middle of this burglary: entering my house
as though for the first time, struck
with the present moment. I can feel
this breath, this hand's touch, these new, hot tears
falling slowly as airships do,
as water does from a flamingo's throat.

The Salar de Uyuni is a salt lake in southern Bolivia,
a volcanic region also boasting multicoloured lakes full of flamingos.

THE MATHEMATICIAN

From his window, he could see snow falling as the fractals
he couldn't see but which he relied on being there.

How could he predict numbers lost at the far end of his imagination
like countries so far away he'd never make it to them?

He sensed a shadow falling, heard a soft thump of snow
and, then, a crack of glass. Below, against the conservatory, an icicle

as pure as an organ pipe, fat as a stalactite made of diamond,
had shattered into its pieces of supercooled clarity.

He thought of her skin: it was as translucent and seductive of light
as ice. It was impossible to talk to her.

On a sheet of paper, he wrote the first of a series of equations:
numbers teaming up as water does, irresistible to itself in the cold,

numbers running through snow like the parallel tracks of a sledge,
and soon his page was filled with their shorthands,

their constructs and passwords. Over on the other side
of the horizon, houses began switching on their lights against the dusk

and he also reached for his lamp. There were some things
of which he could be certain. The rest was love.

HOW IT IS WITH THE CIRCLE

I

Actually it's just a line, but all points
are equidistant from the centre,
without distortion, and that's what makes it
special. Contained by and within that line
are all the attributes of circularity:
the infinite exactitude of **p**,
a circumscribed, two-dimensional disc
too correct to be a moon or an eye,
but sure enough to be a wheel. It's a special
kind of curve, then. Not the curve of a skull
or a country's anxious border. It's starker
than that, less porous, unbreached and a pair
of compasses can swing a black lead
circle on a page pretty double-quick.

II

But we haven't come nearly far enough.
What does a circle become if you puncture
it? All curves and arcs, sections
of construction, lines and roads and scars.
Did Euclid even consider this? Tiny
arcs rejoining to make circlets
which wander off like untethered balloons,
hopeful as helium, for a moment
like soap bubbles carrying their own rainbows.
And the insides seeping out, all that
was circle, into the circumambient
messiness of air, the unpredictability
of blood and time. How it is that flesh wants
to be something else – how it wants to be more.

Carole Bromley

THE HOMECOMING OF SIR THOMAS WYATT

When Sir Thomas returned from Italy
bearing the sonnet, his wife gave him a cold
welcome. She'd had a pinnyful of roundelays
and epics, of his naked foot stalking
in her chamber at all hours declaiming
Sir Patrick bloody Spens and now this.
She'd been hoping for Chianti, one of those models
of the leaning tower or at least a decent bunch
of grapes. And he'd been so irritatingly cock-
a-hoop. Men are like that. Have to plant
their little flags. She didn't let on though,
just thought 'Oh well at least it's short', folded
her arms and gave him a look like Jack's mum
when he brought back that fistful of beans.

THE LAST TIME

The last time I saw my father
he was sitting at a formica table
with two other elderly gentlemen.
All three were wearing blue plastic bibs
and a nurse in a sweater was spooning in
rice pudding and strawberry jam.
It was like one of those tea-parties we had
for dolls. You'd prop them up on chairs
and tell them to be good. They never picked up
the cutlery, or spoke, or swallowed
a mouthful of the biscuit and water pudding
you'd lovingly prepared. In the end
you'd drift outdoors to play on the swing
and, for weeks, picked bits of food
from nostrils, ears, tight rosebud mouths
and the dolly cardigans grandma made.

AWAY

Back home my father is having a brain scan.
He's afraid they'll find something
and lock him up. I am admiring a view
in Umbria, looking out over tiles
shaped like hotel curls of butter.

I have left that other me behind. They say
it could arrive any day. *Domani* perhaps,
or *dopodomani*. The airline has a new scam
to cut costs. It leaves your luggage at Stansted.
Surely it should be enough to deposit you
beside a pool with what you stand up in,
a passport, a few hundred euro,
a breeze in the olive grove, a lizard on the wall?

After twelve hours you can buy essentials.
By then you'll have made a mental list
of all the things you can't live without:
sunscreen, fresh underwear, a towel, a hat.
So little to hang on to what you know.
You can do without the pedal-pushers,
the books, that necklace from Australia.

The sky is every different shade of blue,
white almost, where it meets the mountains
I can't photograph. I have no palette
to mix the greens of cedar, bay and almond,
no fine tip to trace a criss-cross orchard,
that avenue of cypress leading to a farm.

They will be sliding my father out now
from a machine like a mortuary drawer.
They will unhinge his visor, let him go,
then start to examine the tell-tale gaps
where memories were; the pier at Saltburn,
the cliff-lift, the way we pressed our noses
on the glass to watch the sea slowly rise
to meet us, slate-grey edged with white.

Claire Crowther

UNTITLED

Single bed. Tall brown lidded
      bin with a foot-press handle.
            White porcelain sink. Deluxe
soap dispenser. Alcohol hand rub.

Orange rubber-tiled floor. Uncontrollable
      curtain reacting over and over
            to a breeze sniping in through
the horizontal slit of an open window.

A high shelf on wheels covered with jugs,
      tiny pink square sponges on sticks,
            cc measures, a blank menu
choice dated tomorrow, Vaseline,

Sou Son body crème, Chanel perfume spray,
      a stack of disposable grey papier-mâché
            hats to vomit into, a half-moon
insert for the chin cut out.

NUDISTS

In the home of the naked, glass is queen.
A rule of sunlight on his left shoulder.
Her forearms hide a Caesarean scar

and a tied net curtain tries
to billow towards thighs that stray apart.
It serves a surprise to passers-by.

Nakedness is not the revelation
of glass. No less opaque than neighbours,
especially after dark when she loosens

the long hair of voiles. He stops talking,
notices that the window is hung with one
slant reflection of them both, framed.

THE WYVERN

They're millinery, roofs, pinned with cranes.
Or dirty sweatbands, the sweeps of concrete
topping blocks. We bang the slats, kneeling
above the Carphone Warehouse, unroll felt
like a black towel.

The boys say
once I'd have been forced to stay down there,
on the pavement, selling eggs and heart-cakes.
Wrong. There would have been women, hammering,
smelling this smoke from a bitumen bin chimney.
The female dragons.

Me, I carry a hose of fire.
I can stand to walk the metal sky
and land on scaffolding like pigeon shit.
I steer by the blue reins of the Wharf.

Two of us roll up the material
to the beginning again, lay it out more slowly.
I flame each turn. In the days of smocks,
I'd have been drunk from scurvy grass ale
like the boys around Wandsworth Plain
sobering up on saloop, made of cuckoo flowers.

EMPIRE

It was all Latin to us,
        the way the box hedge
                tore through a white dress
of convolvulus arvensis.

Buxus sempervivens.
        We looked the lot up
                in a coffee table book,
Familiar Wild Flowers.

Toad flax and poppy
        went for a strategy
                of abundance that year
we moved in

but only watercoloured
        the tough old box.
                The successful cohabitees,
in the end, were drab,

dressed with London cool.
        Ajuga reptans,
                named by Pliny
for its power to drive away

who knows what,
        cowered, bore
                only seven or eight
flowers to the head.

Other labiates,
        dead-nettle and betony
                and the supposedly graceful
festucca elatior,

cramped under wicker fingers
        that could slit hands.
                Your eyes, once.
You tried to dig it out.

Its roots are infected
        by some virus
                that turns the clay soil
around the stems to cement.

The tiny eyes of its leaves
        flash open each year
                among dog grass,
dog campion, dog roses.

LOST CHILD

Scrape the ditch that takes Hob's Moat
to Hatchford Brook. Look through oak roots,

the horse field, uphill to Elmdon.
Is she hiding behind that sky-blue Lexus?

Shout toward the airport. Planes rise
and fall as if ground were a shaking blanket.

Up there, the air hostesses smile.
Inflate your own life-jacket first.

The small original airport building stands
apart, a mother at a school gate.

Pearl was playing quietly alone.
My ear is like a shell the wind swept.

Patrick Early

THE WINDHARP

Barbara Hepworth writes to her lover Ben
Nicholson about her sculpture 'Spring'

Stuck on a headland between two seas,
the wind fidgeting across sodden fields,
beneath one's feet, a rotting forest
laid over blue clay – you are right, Ben,
it is an odd place for a garden.
Ever since you went away, the rain
has been falling through the air
sideways – we step around sheets
of lying water. They reflect the clouds
with just a touch of blue pigment
which quickly dissolves. A tractor
drumming out in the lane is driving me mad!

Today I looked at my egg and thought:
perhaps this is why I feel so jumpy.
The time has come for it to be laid
(if you'll excuse the pun) in its place
in the corner of the garden by the box yew,
but first, I thought I'd ask the wind
to cooperate, lower the waves
down on the shore, iron them out
till they gleam like beaten pewter –
a certain amount of stillness is required.

And miraculously for an hour or so
the wind dropped, and we could hear
one another's voices, I shouted instructions
and the lads manoeuvred our egg
round the fish-ponds. Dear Ben,
if you could see it now after its spring
surgery – the open cavity in the bronze
a hollowed-out perfection –
such a release from liver and lights,
a lifting of all heaviness round the heart!
The wind is picking up again,
and our egg is filling up with green light,
it's breathing, singing like a windharp.

BENEATH THE CLIFF

Following your instructions, I looked down
and saw the quiet cove beneath the overhang
already gathering shadow, a small beach
assembling its privacy before nightfall,
a raked shelf of granite streaked
with green sea moss, a few circling seabirds,
a line of breakers, brown with slurry, flopping
casually ashore, the rock-face shining
and sucking from the retreating tide.

Otherwise not much going on. Stones
placed carefully in a ring, a beer can
and a few charred twigs, where one night
last year lovers came and a fire burnt briefly,
a sorry tangle of blue plastic rope.
Nothing is pristine where we have been,
but this will do: along the huddled line of cliffs
towards Hagg's Head, waterfalls are twisting
in the setting sun, and far out in the bay
a hidden reef is exploding silently.

DREAM OF AISHA

It was your face, Aisha, your face hooded
as always for the street, your high cheekbones
with the criss-cross tattoo.
You often turned up early on the bus from Takkadum,
catching me in pyjamas, throwing up the roller-blind,
letting the scent of jasmine invade the room.
Ça va? Taib. Très bien, Shhshh, Madame sleeping.

Sometimes you caught me feeding the baby,
sat down beside me on the sofa.
I wouldn't let you wipe the milk from the baby's teat
with your henna-stained hands.
You told me you were childless, a widow.
I knew more about babies than you did.

The day you said, *Monsieur, je suis malade.*
I took you at your word, drove you home
to your shack in Takkadum and you asked me in.
I sat on the edge of a roll of sheepskins
sipping mint tea, surprised by your secret opulence,
dazed by the scent of sandalwood.
And the photo by your bed was of me
with the boy in my arms. As I rose to leave,
it began to rain and the rain beat hard
on the corrugated iron roof.

After that you got clumsy, you broke our terracotta plates,
the ones with the criss-cross pattern, not once but twice.
Oh Aisha, we said, *How could you be so careless?*
We have to let you go (with payment of the treizième mois).

Too proud to argue, you drifted away to your people,
to your village, somewhere high in Atlas snow.

THE BURNING OF THE MAPS

Alexander Popovic said he did not really know
why he reached for his matches

when he entered the history room on October 25 1992,
the Year of the Liberation of Vukovar.

Alex told the teacher that it was the maps
that upset him, ordinary school maps

with the different shades and colours of the republics
of the Socialist Federal Republic of Yugoslavia.

He could not get the pictures out of his head –
the lines of irregulars moving through the villages

with the familiar place names – Srem, Baranja, Sombor,
the precise way the bullets prune the blossom

from the apple trees and scar the houses, troops
crawling along the cracks between the territories,

they know the fault lines. And so he began
by burning the map of old Serbia, *Our lovely Kosovo*.

(It's exciting when a map burns – the paper
blackens and curls, for a second you can just make out

the name of a village, a road, a railway line
before it chars and fades.)

I hate the mapmakers, he said, their pens pry
into the history of our feelings,

and then the soldiers come, the roads
are sown with mines, and the bridges sag

on their piles, the people flee across the fields
and the refugees are turned back from the frontiers.

I was glad, Alex said, when the classroom filled
with smoke: since we cannot live together,

the maps must be destroyed, and the towns consumed.
I said to myself – let us begin again.

Since we cannot live in one another's sight,
we'll live back to back in sealed cantons.

Let our villages be nameless. Let our people grow
like apple trees with blank minds.

Lucy Hamilton

from THE LEGEND OF LALLA MAGHNIA

Following the Arab Tradition

Lalla Maghnia is a Muslim warrior-saint, or holy woman, of Algerian myth and legend. She lived, loved, fought battles, married, had children, performed miracles and finally died young in Northern Algeria, where she was the Raj-es-Salin of the religious centre (*Zaouïa*) in Maghnia, the town to which she gave her name. It seems likely that Lalla Maghnia lived around 1750 CE, just at the onset of colonialism.

My source is *La Légende de Lalla Maghnia, d'Après la Tradition Arabe* by A. Maraval-Berthoin (Paris: L'Edition d'Art, 1927). This is a book of 42 chapters in highly poetic prose. It is a dramatic narrative driven by speakers, though the voice remains essentially the same no matter who is speaking. If anything, it has the incantatory and repetitive qualities of a choral work, particularly at the beginning. Each of the 42 chapters tells its own little story and while the narrative is certainly linear, the passage of time between one chapter and the next can be a day, several months or years.

In my sonnet version, for the most part, each poem corresponds to its original chapter. My aim has been not to change any aspect of the story significantly, and in my translation to be generally faithful to the original, especially where I have had to take aspects of Muslim religious practice on trust. Occasional liberties have been taken for the benefit of clarity and/or music, or to privilege the Arab atmosphere over the French.

1

THE DEATH OF RAJ-ES-SALAH

WOMEN	*O my sisters, choke back cries of distress*
	before the homage of those who defend us.
WARRIORS	O you, all-powerful master of our actions
	we name you greatest lion amongst all lions.
SHEPHERDS	O you, all-powerful master of our sheep
	we name you greatest keeper amongst all keepers.
WOMEN	*O my sisters, choke back cries of distress*
	before the humble sentence of those who judge us.
ELDERS	O you, all-powerful master of our counsels
	we name you just and wise at Allah's tribunal.
PRIESTS	O you, all-powerful master of meditations
	we name you torch to illumine our conclusions.
WOMEN	*O my sisters, choke back cries of distress*
	and gag your mouths with solemn vows of silence.

2

THE MOURNING OF RAJ-ES-SALAH

WOMEN	Pull out your hair and scratch your faces so
	your nails will be twice as red: red with henna
	and red with blood. He is dead and O
	my sisters, M'Aout can't count on her white fingers
	his numerous excellent deeds and victories.
	He is dead, the giver of corn and oil and honey
	and O my sisters, stifle your terrible cries
	and grieve with the distant echoes of the valley.
	Our Lion: warrior of all warriors –
	Our Keeper: greatest shepherd of all shepherds –
	Our Wise One: fair and just amongst all elders –
	Our Lamp and Scribe: bringer of light and words –
	Our Master of Believers casts his eyes
	on the enchanted garden of seven rivers.

WARRIORS   On the enchanted garden of seven rivers
our master rests his tired and spent-out eyes
which always guided us with lion power
and now reflect on heaven from where he lies.
O Master of our nightwatch and our battles
we come to you on our fastest horses, faster
than the wind of the South, so your final
sleep will be started with a guard of honour.
Our Master whom we used to fear, whom we
have always venerated like a father,
we name you Tree of the most virile trees.
O you who always loved us as your sons
and taught us courage in the face of fear
we name you Lion amongst the bravest lions.

SHEPHERDS   Although the warriors name you lion of lions
you have been far more watchful than the most
devoted guard dog and kept our sheep from
wild animals and guided them home when lost.
You who understood the voice of our beasts
and invoked their power of fertility,
who cupped in rough and calloused hands the sweet
milk of the household ewes and goats so humbly
and who identified the song of our first
forefathers in the song of the reed flutes,
we name you honoured guardian, fierce
but gentlest man a community could yield.
Keeper of our sheep and lambs and goats
we name you fertile Field amongst all fields.

ELDERS   They name you fertile field amongst all fields
and we the elders who must take decisions
keep our minds agile in spite of being old –

though we renounce the battle-fields of action.
O you who held in your right hand the golden
bullion of truth and in your left the silver
nugget of patience to judge the deeds of men
upon the scales of justice – guide us O Master.
O you whom we gave with great veneration
the holy name and the name of your father
(inherited by him from the Prophet's blood)
we beg you oversee our administration.
And now, O benefactor, we name you Good
before the great and sacred court of Allah.

PRIESTS   Here, before the hallowed court of Allah
we tell the beads of virtues near your body,
these beads that purify men's hands. O Master,
we are the living stones of the rosary
and, reflecting the light of your thought and the lux
of the Mosque forever facing Eastward,
we offer your heart to God on a wisp of cirrus
in thanks for all our living and earthly reward
– we the incense and myrrh of the burning earth.
We are writing the example of your wisdom
and, as the letters in the Book of books,
preserve the good you stood for beyond death
to keep you in the hearts and minds of men
O you, the Torch of torches, Mosque of mosques.

3

LALLA MAGHNIA'S PLEDGE

LALLA   O father, I pledge to keep you living in death.
MAGHNIA   They're still in your house ? emptying the silos
of grain which they have taken from the earth

to fatten the flesh of your waiting flocks: those
warriors, shepherds, elders, priests and judges
awaiting this eighth day of mourning to greet
the heir of Muslim teaching for this age
and to sing at her head as they wept at your feet.
O father, can the arm of a woman defend?
You've taught me bravery and sympathy
and instructed me in pride and humility,
but the task weighs on the one who wears the cape
of command and I sense my whole being bend
to your will to guard my people in faith and hope.

4

THE DEAD WALK IN FRONT OF THE LIVING

LALLA
MAGHNIA

In order that you still speak with me, O
my father, I've placed my steps in yours and I
have been from the house where your holy shadow
is sleeping to the threshold that your body
has just left. Didn't you tell me, father:
The dead walk in front of the living as
sticks before the blind ? Therefore I'd rather
be guided by the past and now as its space
unfolds I see the mirage of memory floating.
Here on the blazing plain this horseman's superb
on his runaway steed. It's you, my father, and in
your arms I'm huddled, tiny and laughing under
the biting wind which tangles your flowing beard
in my black hair as we ride further and further.

Your beard knots with my hair as we ride further
to where the distant mountain-wall approaches –
where the sky descends to kiss the earth

and where, far beyond, your dominion stretches.
Here is the refuge for the orphans and poor –
it's the school where the children learn their writing,
this *Zaouïa* which opens its generous doors
to the sick, weak and hungry. And here, facing
the sky is the porch where *tolbas* meditate
on the Book of books to pass the word of Allah.
And close to this school which you cultivate
with the love of a gardener for his garden
is the mosque where you taught me the Qur'an
since I must follow you in the Zaouïa.

Zaouïa: religious centre, Sanctuary
Tolba: student/pupil or scholar of the Qur'an

5

THE DAY OF EMPOWERMENT

WOMEN	*O sisters, in the house where we have been*
	to bury the sun, another sun has risen.
WARRIORS	On you the daughter of our Raj-es-Salah
	we place command O Lalla Maghnia.
SHEPHERDS	To you the daughter of our guardian
	we give our finest fleece, to you our star.
WOMEN	*O sisters, in the house where we have been*
	to bury the sun, another sun has risen.
PRIESTS	To you the daughter of our holiest man
	we pass his talisman – to you a woman.
ELDERS	On you the daughter of our judge, we place
	his gold and silver scales of perfect balance.
WOMEN	*O sisters, in the house where we have been*
	to bury the sun, another sun has risen.

AT THE ASSEMBLY OF JUSTICE

ELDERS	This shepherd that you see leaning on his stick to help his trailing leg says it was his master who smashed it – in a fit of rage the misdeed didn't merit.
SHEPHERD	For one sheep taken by a jackal he gave me fifty lashes of his cane – may our Lord Allah who sees one and all make you severe on that barbarian!
LALLA MAGHNIA	When Allah the Just sends locusts to his field not *all* his gold will pay to find a servant to chase them away and save the season's yield. You, the thief, have received your punishment.
PEOPLE	*Only Lalla Maghnia's hands can balance* *the gold and the silver scales of justice.*

ELDERS	The merchant you see here has criticized this child for stealing food and wishes him punished since he's just been circumcized – that rite of passage into the age of reason.
MERCHANT	Forget the cake but the leg of lamb is worth an *hassani douro* large and round as the moon and he can't say it's poverty as his mother does embroidery and his father works too.
LALLA MAGHNIA	The mother of this child, the gentle Kadra, is dead and you a grasping moneygrubber will sell some food each day to his bad father to feed this starving little lion cub.
PEOPLE	*Only Lalla Maghnia's hands can balance* *the gold and the silver scales of justice.*

ELDERS	This magistrate complains he paid too dear
	for an aging horse: that he was deceived, set up:
	they filed its teeth to hide the length of its years
	and fed it pepper and liquor to double its gallop.
MERCHANT	He'd owed me twenty douros since his marriage
	and I knew he desperately needed a horse
	but I wasn't cheating when he'd begrudged
	and haggled and refused to pay me as he ought.
LALLA	I can't accept that one who represents
MAGHNIA	authority should be robbed. But he did wrong.
	Take back your horse and he must now dispense
	the twenty – plus one for refusing it so long.
PEOPLE	*Only Lalla Maghnia's hands can balance*
	the gold and the silver scales of justice.

ELDERS	This coffee-coloured girl of mixed Arab
	and Berber descent says that during love-sleep
	Alel here deceived her and slyly robbed
	her of a sequin she'd have given him to keep.
YOUNG	It wasn't *any* sequin. This one was gold
WOMAN	and I was thinking of making it a gift
	to him, a token of my love, but then he stole
	it after love and nothing can heal that rift.
LALLA	Once you made him pay for love and now
MAGHNIA	he's reclaimed it. How much are your kisses
	worth?
	His fine is still too much for a kiss that shows
	the trace of so many other young men's mouths.
PEOPLE	*Only Lalla Maghnia's hands can balance*
	the gold and the silver scales of justice.

ELDERS	This Jew is outraged that his daughter's been
	callously deflowered by unknown men –

	but he allowed her to let her face be seen:
	we told him to Lalla alone that right is given.
JEW	A band of dirty Berbers spoiled my daughter,
	my little girl, my Rebecca, a pure child
	who was going to the well to draw some water.
	O the apple of my eye has been defiled!
LALLA MAGHNIA	Can we capture the eagle which snatches a ewe
	in its talons? Or stop the wind lifting a grain
	from the furrow? Go in peace, knowing that you
	will hence be spared calamity and pain.
PEOPLE	*Only Lalla Maghnia's hands can balance*
	the gold and the silver scales of justice.

Louisa Hooper

THE MOSAICS AT MONREALE

A euro in the slot illuminates
the Testaments. We know the stories, mostly.

See there's Noah, reaching out of his ark
to guide the lion in. His wife and sons
and their wives crowd the windows, faces doubtful.

Above them God sits on his globe and lets
the waters separate revealing sky
and earth. He makes it look easy, creation

a gesture of the hand towards the thing
it loves. Another gesture and the land is filled
with birds, the sea with fish. We are astonished

by the detail, the peacock's long tail feathers,
the stork on tottering legs, the dove, the fish,
I love the fish, heads stretching for the shore,

where their creator sits. Above the door
Eve steps away from a sleeping Adam.

MORNING, LATE AUGUST

Morning, late August, blue sky, and the trees
on the corner of park I can see from
the café, ceaselessly moving; the rhythm
is complex, how each slender branch, each leaf
tickled by some quiet thing that the air
whispers in passing sways sideways or lifts
itself higher a moment testing its
weight on the currents, the buoyancy there.

In the beginning the word, but how many
words would it need to capture one second
of leaves against sky or the dust patterned
on pavements or the air sighing to any
who'll listen: *It's not far to fall* ... breathing
autumn, sweet autumn through the hairs on my skin?

WELSH POPPY

You show me
nothing but yellow
petals, huge

as wings, unfurled
to every gesture
of the wind.

KEATS HOUSE

Fine rain fills the afternoon with lines that
angle easily against the streets you
knew perhaps, heavy with trees, magnolia
blossom. Sunday afternoons curve inwards,
self-contained, like drops of water resting
on the leaves. *If poetry come not as
naturally as the leaves* . . . A wall, beyond's
the house and silence; no one's around.
Inside the rooms are sparse and small; dusty
tokens of a finished life – the books, pens,
lock of hair your sister kept – say little
of the man who never felt *certain of
any truth but from a clear perception
of its Beauty*. The house, if lived in now,
would have some beauty, if toys lay scattered
in the living room, the stairs had carpet,
beds duvets, if windows could be opened
to the garden where the rain's pale silk threads
flowers, grass and trees into itself.

CONNECTIONS

My mobile reminds me of 'A' level
history, the Tudors, specifically
the fashion for exquisite miniature
paintings of lovers. It rests in my hand,
a rectangular jewel, all silver
and black (with the shimmer of lacquer), buttons
backlit with a lavender glow when I
press them to call you. It also takes photos.
I'm gradually collecting a snapshot
for each of my friends. Though the one of you,
eating sushi, isn't your best perhaps,
still for me, it's as if you're that languid
courtier, leaning against a tree, tangled
in tiny white roses. With Hilliard's
skill I would capture the tentative curve
of your mouth, the tilt of your head, your eyes.

Valerie Josephs

CORRESPONDENCE

Our bedroom seems larger than it is.
It feels a long way to the other end

where I climb up to look through
the attic windows onto the street.

On the king-size bed, the opened
square envelope without a stamp

against the deep red quilt.
My mouth is filled with iron filings,

my hands colder than the marble fireplace
and there's a smell of rain.

Through the open window I can hear
the police horses fretting in their yard.

TALKING DRUMMERS

But if I find myself one evening
say, in Dharamsala,
and I smell smoke from a wood-burning stove,
I will be back in a cottage in Shropshire,
seeing the sun rise over the hills,
because I've been up all night
painting the fridge in wood grain;

and I hear a man on the radio
talk about scattering his father's ashes
in Scotland, and when he looked up
saw a golden eagle so near he could see its eyes
open and close, how afterwards it flew away;
once again I'm in Hokkaido
to photograph eagles and the Japanese Crane;

because I see someone who reminds me
of a man I used to know,
I'm back at the Festival Hall with him
and we're dancing to the music of Baaba Maal,
barefoot in his flowing robes,
the talking drummers parade,
everyone is out of their seats,
and nothing separates me from anything else.

DRY

for Mourid Barghouti

The poet came from a dry place.
He drank glass after glass of water
when he read in his native tongue,
knowing he must return
to where flesh dries out like fruit.

I thought of the way water splashes,
the trill it makes in a metal cup,
or how it ploughs a path in dust
when it spurts from a broken pipe.

I will remember that when I am thirsty.

Jenny Lewis

SUR LE PONT DES ARTS

He's looking at a painting of a river and trees,
houses roughly charcoaled-in against a foggy smudge,
a foreground blob that could be a terrier's shadow

or a black hole of invisible light, dark matter
sucking viewers into the artist's untidy mind,
showing them the dissatisfied wife left clearing plates

after a silent Sunday lunch, the son who bores him,
the treasured daughter who ran off to the Pyrenees
with a specialist in sustainable energy

who builds houses out of cartons and solar panels,
where rotas of guests are needed so that they can pee
frequently in order to keep the bathroom lights on.

He's looking at a painting of a river and trees
and thinking about his mistress whom he hasn't seen
for three weeks because she's gone to stay with a sister

he knows she's just invented. Now he's thinking about
his new hat, a smart homburg, and how superior
it is to the artist's floppy hat which is hiding,

probably, a mess of impasto passing for brains.
He's thinking of the terrier, who has just caught up
and is now regarding him with small, adoring eyes.

He's thinking it costs him more to feed the terrier
than buying the new homburgs he prefers to his wife.
He's thinking his mistress is a liar, the artist

an impostor, the artist's wife and son should leave,
the artist's daughter and her husband are complete fakes
and that his own wife is less attractive than a hat.

He's thinking that his terrier is an expensive
excrescence. In fact, he's wishing he was someone else.
He's looking at a painting of a river and trees.

WOMAN BRUSHING HER HAIR

after Degas

In spring, I lived underwater with it –
my dappled hands held auburn hanks
like uncoiled ropes to brush and brush,
while my thoughts drifted upwards
into the pearly green and umber.

By summer, my face was a scribble –
no eyes, a mute mouth. I forced the auburn
from its lair at the nape of my neck,
brushed it over my brow in torrents
with hands like ham bones. By now
I knew I couldn't tame it by myself.

That autumn, I sat on a bed while my maid
tried to groom it. *Does it hurt?* she asked,
as the auburn itself fell like a curtain
over any other possibilities my life held.
She tilted her head and pulled, spilling
a ginger snakeskin over my face and forearms.

In winter, roasting chestnuts, I was caught
in the blaze. My dress became flames.
My maid grabbed the inferno and tried
to brush it out. A jigsaw of shapes held us firmly
in place while in one corner, just in the picture,
a dab of dappled pearl.

BOARDER

Each night I dreamed I was going home,
following my plait down to the train station,
trains whizzed past in their streaming hair of wind,
too fast to catch, and disappeared into the night.

The tunnel stretched out as far as London,
to the mansion flat with engraved glass on its door.
Through it I saw the shadow of my grandmother,
approaching slowly, bent by patterns.

If only my grandmother would reach the door
I could go inside and be safe with my mother.
But the bell ringing was the school hand-bell: I woke
cold, curled like a cockle, my hair newly shorn.

EPILOGUE

You had to mind
a baby, once –

a fractious,
grizzling creature

that had caused its parents
weeks of sleepless nights.

Your method
was to put some music on
then lie down on the floor

and hold the baby
to your chest

where
like a tiny castaway
on a warm island

with limbs relaxed
and every spasm
of colic gone

it slept, soothed
by your breathing:

how I envied it,
and any other child

that had
such consummate
fathering.

Mary MacRae

NEWFOUNDLAND

Suddenly I understand why it's called 'Fall',
the leaves dropping in a soft swoosh
with the first frost, like snow sliding off a roof

and through the big glass doors to the balcony
I see it's starting to snow in slow motion.
Birds emerge through the snow-curtain:

a flicker pulling long black seeds
from the feeder, juncos jumping, but chickadees
won't come until the flicker takes flight.

'Chickadee' – that's what our mother called us
when we were small; later, a word I found
for my daughter. Now, continents divide us

but for today we're sitting together quietly,
just my sister and I in her woodstove-warmed room
watching it snow. Birds, I'm never far from –

give them half a chance and they fly in –
and something in the way the flakes float down
with the dark shapes of birds pressing through them

brings Ben to mind, our cousin who's lived on the streets
for years and thinks he's got his work cut out
keeping all the coloured balls and little sticks

in the air at once, that no less is expected of him,
and whose mother lies awake these snowy nights
praying that he's alive, has a doorway to sleep in.

GLOSE: WATER AND STONE

I am a woman sixty years old and of no special courage.
Everyday – a little conversation with God, or his envoy
         the tall pine, or the grass-swimming cricket.
Everyday – I study the difference between water and stone.
Everyday – I stare at the world; I push the grass aside
      and stare at the world.
                    Mary Oliver, 'Work'

As I drive over a body of land on a ribbon
of tarmac west from Fishguard there's a wolf's castle
of rocks against a sky so wide, so unbroken
that I think for an instant of what I bring, scars
where a breast lived, neck held with a pin, seven
(at least) of my nine lives gone. But this damage
may mend – and light in high places is vast
and unfolds, nameless, like something given.
Most like a sexual pang, a silent pledge:
I am a woman sixty years old and of no special courage.

Stacked in uneven layers, accretions of heat
shimmer above a field and corral horses
in a small group under sheltering alder trees
too far away to see, but I imagine water,
leaves mouthing over a muddy stream,
breeze and breath – God doesn't come into it –
the horses stock still, while straw-coloured stalks
of cow parsley sway under spread loads of seeds,
packed seed-heads whispering their dry secrets
to the tall pine or the grass-swimming cricket.

Motionless, the estuary today, brim-full
and monochrome; each grass-blade mirrors
itself in perfect symmetry, each white gull
floats on its own double. Even the kingfishers
are paired – in air, not water – flying parallel
to the path, two black specks until they turn
under the bridge and there's a flash of blue brighter
than toffee-paper, a miracle as small and usual
as stone breaking water, water polishing stone.
Everyday I study the difference between water and stone.

I'd like to think that part of what I see
when I gaze at the world – those stopped moments
when the breath is knocked away – might be
imprinted on my chromosomes. Then, once
my ninth and last life fails, the cells finally
close and all the atoms disperse, I'll meld
with specks of stone and grass, become fragments
in the dust particulate spinning daily
from dark to light to dark. Sixty years old:
I push the grass aside and stare at the world.

COW PARSLEY

There's a kind of silence like the quiet
of a listening-booth,

somewhere to stay for a while,
an empty cathedral, say,

in the presence of something unknown
and become permeable to,

tinged with colour, cloud,
whatever is indubitably here

and insistent as the Cow Parsley
just come into bloom,

(how lightly the stalk bends
as a bird lands

how quickly it springs back
when the tiny weight lifts),

here, too,
in the spaces between its florets,

in the fretted shadows
under all umbelliferous flowers.

WILD LIFE

the poster promises, rooted in the broken arches
of the Ponte Rotto: Pale Speedwell, Slender Sowthistle
and a Caper seeded by a German Wasp

but all we can see from the new road-bridge
is straggly bushes blowing in the wind
with none of the bright meaning of their names.

Disappointed, we look down the embanked ravine
to where the Cloaca Maxima, the Great Drain
of Ancient Rome discharges into the Tiber

and notice on top, on the flat masonry blocks,
a shelter, a building-site workman's hut, a frame
hung with bits of cloth and blue tarpaulins

so well protected you'd only spot it by chance,
and then I see that some of the cloths are clothes
and the long black stripes are socks hanging to dry,

draped over the side. It's a camp, a castle;
somebody's made his home in this dry vault
high above the river. But how does he live?

And when the Tiber fills its banks, what then –
won't he be swept away, drowned in the flood?
We hurry down the steps to the disused tow-path

and here he's visible, but so far up on his arch
he's hard to see, a small figure eating
and putting food on little trays for the cats.

And, although we're home again, he grows in my mind;
walking under trees that have lost their blossom
I remember a cold Spring, petals and snowflakes

floating down together, almond and plum
with scarcely more colour than snow, how calm that made me,
as if the slow rhythm of their falling

created its own world, aloof, indifferent,
and I think that's what he wants, above the drain,
the ebb and flow of the river, the water's motion,

to feel the pull of the sea at night on the lonely
tow-path and walk to the pulse of wind and rain,
slowing his mind to their relentless measure.

GANNET

This is what I came to look for
    from the rocks at the very tip
        of St David's Head, this bird,

this gannet, so white it reflects the light
    from far out on the open sea,
        one continuous line of body

aimed towards
    the questing head and sharp beak,
        its whole being flowing forward

like Braque's bird, bleached
    and flying over the bay,
        back to Grassholm.

Suppose I could be re-born
    into that frame, what might I find
        in the huge plunge seaward,

the crash of entry, the long
    descent to semi-darkness?
        What fish emerge with?

THE CLEARING

We'd walked a new way in the woods, down
to the next valley then back to where
someone had carved out a meadow after the war

so that coming at it afresh was like a vision
of somewhere unknown, somewhere green
and gold, with the fennel in flower

and the air humming. I half expected
to see cherubs clustered overhead
like swallows with crossed tail-feathers

while we waited the arrival of the angel
and the message. Back home, watching
how a wasp clings to a leaf, sunlight on a wall,

surely, I think, these can bear the weight
of meditation, common things
opening in the mind like a fan painted

with clouds, almond and plum-blossom
and two lovers who've paused halfway across
a half-moon bridge? At night, awake

and listening to a rhythmic patter like footfalls,
I know it's been a good season for owls,
the tawny ones that call and call,

their songs descending in steps to spiral
the house while all else is silent;
by the time their wordless cries

echo inside me, I'm running so lightly
down their rich staircase that I fall and sleep.
But underneath all this there's something else

that won't go away, an abstract and nameless
anguish that needs to hear those soft owl-voices
singing clear in the dark from the far side

of a field or a wood. O life, how we cling to it!
In cold tones, love reconfigures:
each day I wonder what will change for ever.

Lorraine Mariner

TREE

A year today, and I'm standing inspecting a sapling
in Kensington Gardens. Father, this is to be your tree
and though we wouldn't have found it without a map
from the Royal Parks Adopt a Tree, I've a sense of familiarity.

It's closer to Soldier's Walk and you can just see the Round Pond
where you and your brother sailed toy boats together and my mother
says not far from here you made her play cricket, she bowled
to an oak, you batted with your black city gent umbrella.

Later we will walk to the sunken garden, then to the street
where you grew up, not the house, that would be too much
but Aphrodite's Taverna to toast Greece your team's victory
because dad, we supported them so well they've won the cup.

After you died I worried about my love for you, where would it go?
Eating stuffed vine leaves I think I know it's in the trees,
in the wood that could make a coffin, a ship, a pair of goal posts,
in the trunk of an ash we hope will grow, high as a cathedral

high as a long ball soaring above the Portuguese turf
kicked by a hero before a sea of fans in his blue and white shirt.

MY BEAST

When I was a child I worried
that when I got my chance to love a beast
I would not be up to the task and I'd fail.

As he came in for the kiss I'd turn away
or gag on the mane in my mouth
and the fair-haired prince
and the dress that Beauty wore
on the last page of my Ladybird book
would be lost to me forever.

But now I see that the last thing my father
driving home late from work
would have on his mind is the gardens
flashing past and he would never stop
to pick a rose for one of his daughters
and if some misfortune such as

his Volvo reversing into a beast's carriage
did occur and I ended up at the castle
as compensation, the beast would probably
just set me to work cleaning and I'd never
look up from scrubbing a floor and catch him
in the doorway admiring my technique.

Still, as I've heard my dad say,
he and his children may not always
be brilliant but we always turn up,
and in time when the beast comes to realise
that I haven't tried to escape
he'll give me leave one Sunday a month

to visit my family and access
to his vast library, and in bed at night
reading by the light of a candle
I'll shut another calf-bound volume
and hear its quality thud
with something like happiness.

LIESERL EINSTEIN

That summer waiting to hear about my GCSEs
I worked in an ice-cream kiosk on the beachfront
and met a boy expecting to study maths in London
who had a way of putting Mr Whippy in cones,
and away from the children dripping lollies along
the promenade, I let his fingers do sums on my skin.

Come September I was counting back the weeks,
trying to predict when the multiplication we had been
working on would be noticed, and I could understand
what my new physics teacher meant about the cat
in the box that's just been poisoned which you can't
be sure is dead until you lift the lid and take a look.

Throughout October there was morning sickness and
the cat was running around the house to the screams
of my mother, who called me a slut loud enough
for Mrs Evans and her hard hearing, while my father,
too stunned to remind his wife about the neighbours,
tore up my postcard of Saint Paul's Cathedral.

Now it's September again and I'm back at my desk,
my mother at home with her own second chance,
another summer gone, a new law of motion learnt,
comparing hair and eyes, the way we sometimes cry,
and the boy from the kiosk comes home when he can
and demonstrates that he also has a way with bottles.

Tonight, when you finally slept, I read about Einstein
and how even he with his head for figures could make
the classic miscalculation and get his girlfriend pregnant;
but they gave their daughter away, a wrong answer.
We will work this out. You are simply someone new
among our number that we need to take account of.

MAC

Eating in Regent's Park once more at his suggestion,
the last time that I saw him, I went to find the toilet
and when I came back he was wearing one of those
complicated outdoor pursuit macs, carried in his bag

ready for the rain, and I was amazed it fitted in there
but did not say, just zipped up my showerproof jacket
and hoped it wouldn't put me to shame, which it didn't.
But three months later, standing in another park, listening

and trying to see Radiohead, close to a man who had
the same sort of coat as his, and a wedding ring and a wife
who let her husband stand behind her back with his hands
in the pockets of her mac, it did. And soaked to my skin

walking back to the car, I decided I was going to get myself
a mac and a man like that, who would stand and hold me
by its pockets, regardless of the crap in them which I should
have binned, and I wouldn't get wet like this again.

Barbara Marsh

BECK AND CALL

He arrived in a white Buick, torn leather seats
in the back. Three thousand miles without a map,
he'd headed north towards Quebec. Stopped
outside Bucky's café, downtown Main Street
in Springbok, Indiana, got the car wedged
between a '70s Schwinn tandem bike
and an El Camino, a book about coffins on the bed.

Her name-tag said Rebecca. She held a box
of brown meringues, fresh from the baker next door,
set them on the counter, stuck a Bic ball-point
in her hair, took chalk from behind a bouquet, printed
Today's Outback Specials on the café blackboard.
He looked taken aback, asked 'Am I in Australia?'
and she giggled, her mouth like a little beak. His knees
vibrated like the humbucker pickup on his old guitar
and he hoped the tobacco stains didn't show on his teeth.

He felt like a prince in the house of the Bacchae, noticed
how shrivelled buckeyes flurried around telephone poles,
the tobacco-coloured floorboards bled bone
into the concrete buck where the mat rested outside,
Welcome to Bucky's. He wondered if Australia was so far
after all, a beaker of oil and a fryer on the stove,
Rebecca, the meringues, a baby crawling on the floor,

if he'd be *welcome* even with a bouquet when he drove
the red dirt home, Bic razor in his pocket, the smell
of a bake-off in the village, the house full of drawings
and noise. There'd be Rebecca in her best dress, small things:
a new book he didn't understand, a stormy spell
and a TV programme on Quebec. He would wonder
why he'd stopped in Springbok, Indiana, or if
all those bridges were still burning back in Daytona,
where he'd stolen his uncle's Buick on a bet, scared stiff.

INTERIOR

It is a Wednesday night.
Evinrude, next door's cat,
runs into our house
soon as the door opens,
just a crack and she's in,
a brown streak with her outboard purr.
There's a light on
in the corner, and the shutters
are open, the night air
pulls at the flame on the stove,
makes it stutter,
ruffles the untouched post.
You walk by me
and say nothing. I say nothing back,
pour some wine into the soup.

My mail on the table
is a white stack that's grown
by the day. When I lift it, a clutch
of envelopes slips to the floor,
catches your attention.
As you kneel beside me
there's a second when this
is enough: our hands
as we gather up letters,
the cat as she rubs against my elbow,
the sound of our breathing
when nothing is unsaid.

GREAT-AUNT CONSTANCE

I feel heavy with years that seem to have come to this picture
of a young woman in a winter coat, contemplating
an ashtray on a table. It was the 1930s. Little money,
fewer jobs. An era, a relative I never knew.

I walk back and forth in the rooms of ancestors, climb
their ladders, even as I stiffen to the shouts of children outside
who fuck with my concentration and my aching broodiness.
I have a coat that same Copenhagen blue.

New York City is a communal photograph album,
memories blending until I'm not sure
what I remember and what I've only heard about
You don't miss what you've never known. Not true.

My knuckles are red with cold. In the mirror my eyes
look so tired. I crumple a tissue into the ashtray,
turn to the window. That new building blots out the skyline,
but around the corners a little light cuts through.

SUNLIGHT IN A NEARLY EMPTY ROOM

i.m. M.D.

Except for that spot where the sun shines
through the window, the floor is cold.
You could stand there until the world moves
that bit farther and the light grows

too thin to warm. You're all bones now –
your body has abandoned you in this.
There's no bed any more, only the steel chest
of drawers, taking up a whole wall.

A pencil rolls across the floor.
You follow it, you and your bones,
your empty flesh, your cold hands.
You put your ear to the door.

It's like standing beside a seashell –
there's the sea, whishing, whispering,
Come in, come in, come in. But you're
already in. The sea is outside, surely.

Karen McCarthy

SCATTERING THE ASHES

You died in the back of a Cairo cab,
quick and unceremonious. A heart attack.
Your faithful Nikon monocled to an eye that scanned
landscape for the angle of edifice at every turn.
Rooms of holiday snaps remain, peopled
by a sprawling family of buildings.

We shipped your body home:
from Egypt's tombs to Highgate catacombs.
A skewed trace on the map of Jewish migrations.

All I can see is the black umbrella clicking shut.
Light devoured and spat out on to paper.
Looming towers, green-nostrilled gargoyles
carved in stone; and us two kids jostling with
cathedrals, forgotten monuments, even offices,
for space in this already crowded frame.

Later, like all good teenagers,
we learned to scowl out from sullen
hedges of hereditary eyebrows,
as mum smiled on in the face of it all.

At home, Mozart vied with Marley:
a generational impasse, with you
on longwave, my dial tuned to FM.
You were older than the other dads.
Bored by football. We all took the piss out
of your accent. And the way you liked garlic
– with everything. Besides, you were busy
planning the new metropolis, erecting
vast urban monoliths for London County Council.

A world reconstructed to withstand bullets, gas, Hitler.
Having survived all that, how could you
ever be sure of anything that lived
and breathed and faltered, like we did?

THE BEACH AT CLOVELLY

Although Melissa 'dropped' her birthday cake in a strop
it didn't matter because we'd had such fun walking up cliffs
with the wind on our faces.
Wavey-Davey brewed tea on his camping stove
and everyone gathered round him as if he was a bonfire.
We drank like Vikings, squeezing red wine out of a silver bladder,
courtesy of Larry who retrieved a shimmering dead pheasant
from a tunnel in the rocks.
Manda wanted to look like Marianne Faithfull in *Girl on a Motorcycle*
– and she did.
Gary filmed everything on his Super 8,
while Jean stalked about in a black gypsy hat.
People took photos of people taking photos.
Bim was quiet.
The tide was coming in.

THE WORSHIPFUL COMPANY OF
POMEGRANATE SLICERS

Before you know this apple of many seeds,
this globe of islands and seasons and blood,
it does not matter whether your knife
is serrated. All that matters is the cut, the spill,
a taste so sour only salt can make it sweet.
At its heart revealed: a glistening star.

Punica granatum you are the hidden star
of David: six hundred and thirteen seeds
in the white of the aril, each one a sweet
boiled red by a meticulous God whose blood
seeps blue on sands where Bedouins spill
stories like goat guts from the tip of a knife.

Orion went hunting with his dog and his knife.
He carved Side's sun-skinned city as his star.
She shone so bright Queen Hera vowed to spill
her calyx crown and scatter her limbs like seeds.
Goddesses! You've never seen such a blood-
thirsty lot; a rival's head tastes sweet.

Gods are no better. When Hades lured sweet
Persephone deep underground, no knife
was needed: just a contract signed in blood,
a tempting daffodil and the garnet star,
his jewel of winter. She ate six seeds,
then let all she ever dared desire spill

on to her tongue; let pink, sharp juice spill
over lips stained purple with sweet, sweet
abandon. But before too long bitter seeds
of doubt began to grow and Hades' knife
was a smile that eclipsed her guiding star.
Demeter: her light, her source, her blood.

Come inside! Wet your head in the blood
of the fruit, let the exhilaration of wine spill
into your throat. Breathe in, inhale the star
dust. Pull the pin, explode every sweet
secret, watch each one blaze across a knife-
slashed sky. Soft earth will catch the seeds.

Slice the circle while your blood runs sweet.
All you will spill with your sickle knife
is a star from a cluster of seeds.

David Penn

TRIAL AT A BUS STOP

Dear Miss Strand,
I believe they're your girls in the red
and black? I saw some earlier today,
assembled round the bus stop opposite
the Harvester on Beulah Hill. I thought
I ought to tell you what was going on.
It's been a windy day, and days
like this induce a sort of skittishness,
I know – and I was once a teenager . . .
The leaves, red-ochre, brown, were rolling
round like overflow from pirate treasure,
gold that had escaped and hoped to creep
unnoticed through the grass. The girls
were all absorbed in circling round
each other in a complicated spiral, like
a time-lapsed opening rose or galaxy
in miniature. And at the centre
was a tiny girl, a black girl with
a red beret, round spectacles
and dimples that made mischief round
a gap-toothed smile. Her two front teeth
would loom like tigers' teeth and threaten
everything: the universe, herself included.
She was chubby, you might say, not fat,
full-cheeked, her hair in ribboned bunches
roaring from her head like smoke.

Whenever any bus drew up
you'd see the most extraordinary thing:
the girls would swarm around it like
a clan around a giant hog
and hammer on the doors. The buses, though,
are always full that time of day –
with other kids just out of school –
and so the drivers (God be with them)
wouldn't let them on. The girls
would fall back on themselves, a self-
enfolding wave, but this girl ran
at every bus and pressed some buttons
on the side that flung the doors
wide open – buttons that are only
for emergencies of course. You saw
the drivers cursing from their cabs,
but there was nothing they could do.
The girls all yelled when she came back
to them: 'Again! Again!', by this stage
having dropped all thought of getting
on a bus by any means. Each time
the doors slammed back it was as if
she'd opened up a wound in some
huge beast, or was provoking some
enormous dragon, playing round
its jaws. And these were double-deckers,
tall enough to scrape the trees.
They dwarfed us all like siege machines.

No other adult at the bus stop
did a thing, I have to say.
They fidgeted as if it wasn't happening,
checked watches, clouds, their feet.
I hardly knew myself what we
should do. I made a move as if
to stop the girls but felt more like
a stranded carp than anyone who could
command authority. I stood there,
brave in my imagination – folded arms,
expanded chest – but having no
effect: some village bobby of
the nineteen-fifties, stepping from
a time-machine to find himself
invisible. What shall we do?

'We are the AY bee CEE-ee MI-nors . . .' we sing,
sit down, lean forward in our seats and wait.
A little queue has formed at the steps leading up
to the stage. The manager stands, tuxedoed, bald,
neck reaching from his collar like the boom
of a crane. 'Harrumph.' He taps the microphone.
'All right, you three, come up. It's all your birthdays,
is it? You are?' 'Michael. And I'm TEN.' We cheer.
'And you, son?' One by one they all address
the held-out microphone as though they're drinking
from a silver cup, then he turns and bellows:
'Right, come on' – arms up conducting, sleeves
to the elbows - 'Haaappy Birthdayyyy to you, Haaappy . . .'
'Who are we?' 'ABC Minors.' 'Who are we?'
'ABC . . .' 'Enjoy the show.' He strides
to the wings and waves, his spotlit shadow rippling
down the curtain as it lifts. The tunnel round
the Warner Brothers logo looms and gapes
then Loony Tunes: Bugs Bunny bites a carrot
and we bang the arms of our chairs. King
of The Rocket Men begins, part nine – a flashback
chops through scenes, a shiny grown-up blonde
is carried off from bullets by a man
in dark grey overalls with rockets sparkling
from his back. She wriggles and screams. We fidget
through the kissing, then when fighting starts again
we hammer heels against our seats - warriors massing
for a battle, drumming spears against their shields.

A WOMAN OBSERVED IN A PUB

The woman with the whipcord hair
does a bee dance from the loo.
She slow-zigzags across the floor,
uncertain of her step – as though
she's realised she's a tightrope walker
suddenly.

Foundation smeared like chalk,
black cherry lipstick, auburn hair;
her cheesecloth shirt, worn jeans
and satin bomber jacket
hang as loosely as a circus tent.

And at her table,
there's her boyfriend, holding court,
his gold-ringed fingers spread like
palace gates, his silvered glasses
too absorbed to point her way.
She sets down like a bird
and lights a cigarette, and stares at the wall
and talks towards it, nodding.

Like a puppet balanced by a leaden weight
inside her skull, she moves her cigarette
between her mouth and the space
in front of her, then leaves it
like a short white needle, dripping wraiths.
And as she leans
towards the invisible friend,
she holds a hand to him across the table,
and the boyfriend turns mid-tale
and freezes, watching.

The invisible guide is listening now,
and when he listens, he really listens
and when he speaks
he must be saying something good,
because she nods, and smokes,
and takes it all in.

Derrick Porter

AFTER THE STORM

(for Elizabeth)

On Dalrachie Pool,
under rings of darkening cloud,
a tink, like a soft note, dropped onto water.

Looking up from the keep-net,
hung limp like a scarecrow's pocket,
I lifted my collar against a turning wind

. . . tink, tink, tink, followed by
an irregular rhythm that beat down
as if musicians were leaning into each other.

Then the mellow softness of a sax
blew in on the low cloud
holding me to that spot, until the first notes

of morning awakened me
to a singing of water . . . and salmon rising
like merchants at the start of their trade.

THE CARRIERS

They were a strange breed who carried in our coal,
peering out through circles of dust
and grunting through grind of gritted teeth,
bodies pressed hard against the cart;
the horses reeking of hot urine, shaking
their metallic livery, each colossal shoe
echoing the stamp of each wearied tread.

Later, men drove the horses, deaf and broken,
past our door en route to the slaughterhouse,
their yellowing eyes already carousing sleep.
Like old cave drawings they ingrained their time
while stumbling slowly towards departure.
Few now know the ways of horses.
And none have passed our door in years.

SYDNEY AND OTHER PLACES

A stranger at the station asked about one
of two stickers on the side of my travel bag:
When were you last in Australia?
Forty-one years come November, I told him.

We shared memories of Sydney Harbour,
its butterfly boats and aquatic shell
later to become the Opera House. When he said
he'd left Australia for America, I almost shouted *Me too!*

although the name of the National Park
where we'd first seen the Bee Gees
and the Beatles perform escaped us.
But not the 'Blue' and 'Snowy' Mountains.

As his train came to a momentous stop
he rose, then, stepping aboard, turned
and pointed his stick at my travel bag:
You know, he said, *I've never been to Bournemouth.*

AS THE DAYS PASS

Who will remember our fine phrases
tell of their meeting us on a train
                              to Marseilles
or struggling under the shadow of a basilica
to decipher a Roman platitude,
    recall that our black shoes
        had brown laces
and on our lapels
                  hairs
    that glistened more brightly
than our own.

O heart, were we to write
        as one of the great French poets
let it be as Guillaume Apollinaire,
                        plucking as he
the pure light from that little square
close to St-Germain-des-Prés
        where he found the tumblers
and the miraculous child:

then, with the tenacity of his louse
        that 'won't let go'
                    write on
    till we had produced a *Pont Mirabeau*

or sit below the silver Seine
                    in a dream of desiring so.

Shazea Quraishi

SKYROS

I live near the place with the honey.
It's always Spring here. I sing
and cook, bare and brown
or in my purple dress.

In the day there are birds
with so many different songs, I can't choose,
and at night, the brass shimmering of goat bells
leads me into sleep.

Maybe tomorrow I'll go
down the road with the purple rock and fig tree at dusk
to find the beekeeper's garden, dripping
with milk and humming.

STILL LIGHT

You picture your mother as a tree
– somehow that makes it easier.
A silver birch, undressing
unhurriedly, as though days were years,
while a fine rain plays
like jazz in her hair. She drops
her fine, white leaves
one by one. Her branches
are almost bare now. See,
how beautiful she is against the darkening sky.

The woman who was not me sat down in the chair indicated by the doctor. She started to speak and proceeded to come unglued, to let go and flow into the crevices and folds of the rough brown fabric of the chair, stopping just short of ending up at the good doctor's feet.

The doctor, whose name was Anne, put out her hand to place it on the woman there, and said how she liked to think of all the mothers alone at home all over the world as hundreds of thousands of little lights shining in the dark.

ALL THIS TIME

I've been living the wrong life.
I stepped out to bring in the milk
15 years ago

and now I see
I'm in the wrong house.
Who is this man

with the plaster dust on his hands?
What are these children doing in the kitchen?
The boy is skinny, smells

of goat, mixes Cheerios
and Alpen in his cereal bowl. The girl
reminds me of a jug

my mother had,
the china so fine, the milk shone
a blueish light through it.

Where are my bright
skirts, my heavy silver rings,
the red in my hair?

Kathryn Simmonds

LEFTOVERS

Lit like a tabernacle, the fridge
does not contain a miracle
but only bits of bits in bowls.

The cat meows; the soft drum
of her belly beats a pang for rollmop,
milk slops, bacon rind.

She'll have to wait: life is full
of hanging around, I tell her.
(Mung beans? Ratatouille? Skate?)

The bachelor across the way
falls on his knees, reaches in the dark
for jars, while next door

lovers offer one another hearts
and cauliflowers, or pasta shells
the shape of babies' ears.

Upstairs, someone whose post
I once received weighs up
his appetite for take-away, walks

a Yellow Pages round and round
the hard wood floor.
In time, a scrap of moon appears.

I haven't seen the muffin man
for years, or met a pieman
going to a fair, I've only stood here

talking to the Tupperware,
the dining table laid with light,
old receipts and unpaid bills,

working out a way of using up
these failing greens, a recipe
for half a weightless aubergine.

SEAHORSES

Dawn: like 18th-century
coquettes they court each other
crowned with coronets, blushing
pale yellow or vermilion,
linking their prehensile tails;
floating flirts, pot-
bellied dancers

defecating in a swirl,
riding through the themes of eel-
grasses, mangroves, water weeds;
dainty freaks, slowest swimmers
of the sea. Camouflage is
all they have, their
charm to fend off

Chinese chefs who pluck them from
their beds and drop them into
glassy soups, or fan their
bodies over canapés.
Shamans powder them to cure
impotency
or a wheeze, and

trinket peddlers pinch them too,
dry them in the sun until
they're fossilised, set them in
the man-made amber of a
paperweight, or string them by
the seraphs of
their necks like slight

Lolitas. Miraculous
medals. Meanwhile, we shadow
them, peering from our darkness
at their curlicues of light
like aquarium voyeurs
biding our time.
Jewel thieves. Hunters.

REASONS TO BE CHEERFUL

Cross-stitching in the fingers of old women
who have loved, and council flats in cherry light
which knows no class distinctions.

Patients gulping jelly in the hospitals,
and varnished floorboards splitting water
into glassy baubles. Bumblebees

at work or profligate, and fountains
in the middle of the city where the hearts
of artichokes are being eaten in a snack.

The language of the women on the train,
the way it made them sift the air
with power to divine the dreams of mice.

Rocking chairs. The tablecloths at Ronnie Scott's,
the orange sunflowers on your bed,
seahorses living their exquisite lives in miniature,

and Stevie Wonder being born.
The fact that someone must have improvised
before the tambourine, and *over easy*

is a fried egg giving up
its golden yolk without distress;
that bowling balls are solid molecules of hope,

and Margot Fonteyn danced at fifty-six
as Juliet, long-haired and loved by Nureyev.

ANGELS AT REST

Through the bracken and the overgrowth they come,
huge iridescent sandaled feet,

hoisting each other up, then sprawling in the trees
like celestial tigers. They detect

aspirins crunched like ginger-nuts in nearby towns,
but stay put, tired of hovering

at bedsides (the wallpapers ever in bloom), tired
of collecting where cars collide,

preferring this, the graveyard's mustard light, the gnats,
late summer turning over like the dead.

It doesn't last, of course. A woman picks through grass,
bluebells wilting in her fist, finds a stone

and bends, predictably, begins to cry. The angels sigh,
sad for the smallness of the living,

the living, with their expansive novels and their bluebells,
their millions of ideas and manifestos,

their billion worries too (free falling aircraft, armies of irate
diseases) more real to them than flame-

lit trees. The angels beat their wings and contemplate
the gnats instead – specks

of almost nothing, massed like clouds, their unseeing eyes,
their fathomless, microscopic hearts.

THE DEAD ARE DEAD

And still we long to break their silences, just as we did
when they were alive (*a penny for your thoughts*).

Did I say they? I'm talking about you of course,
about the way I thought I'd spin and spot

you slipping through the kitchen door with one
last word, or squint and see your pale double

in the mirror mouthing a departing gag. But not
a whisper or a wobble. My Private Eye smokes

under streetlamps while I sleep, ready to return
another snap, a fragment of your speech.

The dead are dead, of course, so why is it I leave a tape-
recorder running in the dark to wake and play

back sibilance, which might be someone straining
to make sense. Why do I find I'm daydreaming

of mediums with microphones, a hall of strangers trooping
in with restless ghosts beneath their overcoats

as if they'd swallowed up their loved ones whole.
'Does the initial J mean anything to you? She tells you

to be careful of your back. She's happy and she sends
you love.' Why do I want a postcard scribbled from

'the other side'? *Wish you were here.* Full of platitudes
and sound advice. Are all ghosts sentimentalists? Are you?

Saradha Soobrayen

LIKE COLD AIR PASSING THROUGH LIPS

I shall think of you as my ventriloquist,
lying under the cedar trees. Your lips
unreadable, my mouth daydreaming:
journey, draining, geranium.
My head heavy more with rhymes than sleep,
resting on your arm, near the shadow's edge.
The fragrance of wood neither green
nor brown, but shallow blue.
Your compliments lodged in me
like harvest mice nesting under leaves,
foxgloves at our feet, the north winds singing.
My ear as dumb as corn and too far gone,
to catch your heart closing like a gate behind me.

ON THE WATER MEADOWS

I blame the twilight for coming too soon,
not allowing enough time for you
to drown without dying. And now
the water boatmen skate on the skin
of water; we should have practised
how to breathe. Instead we undressed
each other slowly: middle names, first
loves, spiders, toads and newts. Taking our
time to visit every corner, all the while
knowing we would soon run out of self.
I want to ignore the silver scar
on your left retina: the imprint of an iceberg,
those places you were yearning for: Bermuda,
Pacific, Icelandic waters. Confident diver
that you are, land was never your best side.
What remains is the space around
your hands, their quietness, and at the tips
of fingers the faint hum of blue.

QUESTIONING THE INVISIBLE STITCHING

Don't make me reach for you
with the anxiety of a first time traveller,
in the spirit of a truant, unable to love.
Now that the sparkle has gone, this poem remains
sleepily in my mind, breaking into snippets.
I'm lost in this twilight, unlike you, unwinding
our threads, mending holes in warm pockets of air
or magic. So much was up your sleeve: the birth of books,
musing on whether a rhyme equals hard work
and the art of disappearing. A sleight of hand and I am left
under a spell, with some minutes not yet uncoiled,
making you more precious. These hours are written
while the air is thick with thinking errors. A fleeting chill;
a moth dashes across my eyes, back and forth.

A moth dashes across my eyes back and forth
while the air is thick with thinking errors – a fleeting chill
making you more precious. These hours are written
under a spell, with some minutes not yet uncoiled,
and the art of disappearing; a sleight of hand. And I 'm left
musing on whether a rhyme equals hard work
or magic? So much was up your sleeve: the birth of books,
our threads mending holes in warm pockets of air.
I'm lost in this twilight, unlike you, unwinding
sleepily in my mind, breaking into snippets.
Now that the sparkle has gone this poem remains
in the spirit of a truant. Unable to love,
with the anxiety of a first time traveller, ∗
don't make me reach for you.

THE MORNING AFTER

With not one look or wink or smile,
we sit for breakfast. A bowl, a mug,
a spoon wait for my mouth to open.
I watch as you rise to rearrange
the shutters, tapping out the chinks of light,
as if they were bars of a glockenspiel.

You like the mornings slow with sleep
still near. Yesterday the sun was wide-eyed
and you wouldn't slip off your hood,
wouldn't let me say 'I love you'. The phrase
drifted towards the clouds as we lay
with the primroses and buttercups.

But I kept my point, not the whole
words, just the vowels: the 'o'
and the 'u'. Kept them through our
greedy night till this exhausted
morning, past the first glint
on your eyelash and well after
ten past nine, when cold yellow
stretched across the bedroom wall.

I heard the vowels when you pulled
off the covers, spilling the orange juice.
They are here as I sit and hold
my tongue. The bowl and mug and spoon
are waiting to catch them. And as you plop
out your teabag and drip egg yolk down
your hand, the 'o' and the 'u' are free-falling,
seven degrees east, from your left cheek.

MY CONQUEROR

She circles me with her Portuguese compass
and settles just long enough to quench her thirst.
She discards my Arabian name *Dina Arobi*,
and calls me *Cerné*, from island of the swans.

With the hunger of a thousand Dutch sailors
and a tongue as rough as a sea biscuit she stakes
a longer claim and makes herself comfy,
bringing her own Javanese deer, pigs and chickens.

Defending her lust for breasts and thighs, she blames
the ship's rats for sucking the Dodo from its shell.
Looking past my ebony limbs, she sees carved boxes
and *marron* hands at work stripping my forests.

She renames me in honour of Prince Maurice
of Nassau. A good choice, sure to scare off pirates
keen to catch a bite of river shrimp, flamed in rum.
Disheartened by cyclones and rat bites, she departs.

For eleven years, I belong to no one. I sleep
to the purring of turtledoves. Sheltered by a circle
of coral reef, my oval shape rises
from the coast up to the peaks of mountains.

A westerly wind carries her back. She unbuttons
her blue naval jacket slowly and takes me.
I am her *Île de France*, her *petit pain*.
She brings spaniels. She captures *marrons*

who are pinned down and flogged, each time they run.
She takes her fill in Port Louis, shipping casks
of pure sweetness to the tea-drinking ladies of Europe.
Young Baudelaire jumps ship on his way to India.

His stepfather wants to cure him of 'literature'.
Once a poet makes his mark, no tide can wash away
his words: 'Au pays parfumé que le soleil caresse'.
And what can I say, he was so delicious!

Sadly sweet Baudelaire soon finds himself
in such a profound melancholy,
after seeing a whipping in the main square,
after two weeks he sails to France, leaving me

a sonnet. With the pride and jealousy of
the British Admiralty she punishes me
with her passion for corsets, sea-blockades
and endless petticoats wide as the Empire.

The oldest profession is alive and thrives
in my harbours; strumpets and exports, cross-
dressing captains and girls in white breeches.
Boys who like boys who like collars and chains.

She brings a pantomime cast of *malabars*
and *lascars* to my shores. Their passage back
to India guaranteed, if only they can read the scripts.
The cane breaks backs. Tamil, Urdu, Hindi, cling

to their skins like beads of sweat. Hundreds of tongues
parched like the mouths of sweethearts in an arranged
ceremony. She is kind and ruthless and insists
on the Queen's English. At night Creole verve slips in

and makes mischief. Each time she comes she pretends
it's the first time she has landed here, but she soon
becomes bored. Tired of flogging and kicking
the dogs. She doesn't know which uniform to wear.

'I'm no one and everyone', she complains.
'And you have no more distinguishing marks
left to conquer'. She pulls down her Union
Jack; it falls like a sari, around her bare feet.

Marrons: Creole name given to the slaves taken from
Madagascar and transported convicts.
Malabars and Lascars: Hindu and Muslim indentured labourers.
These names are disparaging terms in Mauritian Creole.

Kay Syrad

THE GALLERIST

We are on the slope, our mouths
wanton from the mackerel and
hard-boiled eggs. The men bring
Anya along the path. No, she brings
the men along the path. We look
towards her, the woman who brings
our men along the path, a woman
with high apricot stretched over her
lips. The men gesture towards us.
She stands still whilst the men own
us, we have time to examine her filmy
eyes, the black headband with white
polka dots over henna'd grey hair. 'And
this is *my* wife.' My eyes, for the briefest
longest second, are able to rest in hers.

We follow Anya to the white barn.
Inside, we face six granite monoliths
placed round a square. We feel awe
and we feel cold. Anya stands with
her back to the wall and talks. We listen,
each in turn daring to edge away to
study the granite blocks, aware of
the scrape of our boots. The light
in the barn meets the mica in the stone;
the girders are red, the roof grey.
'Yes, it is cold', says Anya. 'The artist
says to me, as he gets older he gets more
cold. He wishes this to be represented
in his work.' We think of his old bones
cold beneath his skin, how a heart ices over.

We stare at Anya's olive jeans and
listen to names: Long, Lang, Nash,
Leib, Zürich, Woodstock. We let
our eyes draw up the granite columns
once more and file out of the white
barn. Anya is tall amongst us as we
move towards the artist's cottage,
see his paintings on the walls. 'Bauhaus,'
she says. 'All the furniture, Bauhaus.'
In the courtyard a man and a boy
load a grand piano into a horse-box.
The man speaks to Anya in a high
aristocratic moan, we cannot tell
what he says. We walk a high tunnel
of rusting trees, see the empty lake.

Anya brings us along the path to her
house, makes coffee, puts out a single
pastry. We sit at her ash table, our eyes
sneak over the walls, the books. With
the dark coffee on our lips we see
the photograph, a dead person,
blood on his arm and his neck, grainy.
'It is the first photographic still from
television to become art,' she says.
We are impressed and dismayed. We
have brought in our mackerel and eggs
and the men eat. Anya picks at her single
pastry. 'The artist is in Germany', she
says. 'He was homesick for his language.'
We think she was the artist's lover.

The tall elegant Anya with high apricot
lips. She is seventy, her eyes are pale,
she is sixty-five, her eyes are mischievous.
She shows pictures of her Hamburg
Gallery, 1970s: Anya's long legs and
delicate lips, Anya with the artists,
Hockney, Warhol. One by one we creep
up the narrow stairs to her bathroom,
our eye caught first by a poster of
Tracey Emin in the bath, her dark nipples
floating on the paper's surface, then
by a Mapplethorpe: glistening hips,
a graceful penis. On her shelves, five
wristwatches, a dozen perfumes, the
John Lennon and Yoko Ono bag.

'Yes, he is homesick, he is tired.' And
cold, we remember, too cold to keep
on loving Anya. 'But tomorrow I go
to the Hunt Ball! I take my tartan
bedspread, drape it round my body,
on top my black jacket and no one
suspects a thing. When first I was in
London I wore my green velvet
curtains to every party. Tomorrow
I am Ambassador's guest, he is gay,
everyone knows it, but always he takes
a woman to the Ball.' I imagine the two
at the Hunt Ball, the Ambassador as
the woman, Anya his male escort, the
Ambassador hung with tartan, green velvet.

CARNIVAL OF THE LAZY KINGS

I see him slow, in orange light, in smoke,
his long black hair sleek and black, see him mourn
the golden float, the lazy klezmer slow
and low, low and slack. And the red plush Kings
are riding high, their golden thrones high and light
as the song unfurls in the feathered black.

Two pierrots propel the float, white and black
on one-wheeled bikes, pull the float long and slow
– a giant's bed with wrought-iron sides. The Kings
swing from a treble clef in golden light –
sway through a tall, a hungry arch, pink smoke
pink on poplar leaves. And I watch him mourn

a love; I love his love, blue-black, I mourn
his love (this orange glow, the Klezmer slow
and lazy, slow and long, the arches black,
the pierrots flying white and high, the smoke
in the leaves, in the poplar trees, the Kings
in plush, in red plush thrones in blazing light).

We move slow and crimson, slow in the light,
following the floats and the rococo Kings
who sing like fish to the silver night. Black
are his shoulders and his long smooth hair, slow
his step, his graceful step, and what I mourn
is love's plush rising in the slow red smoke.

The pierrots gesture in red, through smoke
at a gold wire bird circling in the black,
high as the poplars, high above the King,
those louche and Lazy Kings – and I mourn
my love, his silk black hair sleek in the light,
his step, his lost love floating in the slow

red rising of the night. His love is slow,
it circles long, I long for love, I mourn
the silver dark. The floats are still, the light
above is dazzling bright, my heart is black
and a gold wire bird turns slow in the smoke,
the orange-pink smoke of the Lazy Kings.

I mourn him, long and slow in orange light,
in the flare smoke pink of the Lazy Kings,
mourn his love, long, sleek and tulip black.

DOUBLE EDGE

for Thomas Joshua Cooper

I

Norway. Europe – its north-most northern point
in the Barents Sea: this is where light leaks
from the photographer's hands like milk and streaks
the black rock promiscuously; or moves to anoint

the sandstone crag, as the dark slopes in front
call up the angel, the net of spray that speaks
each time the sea swells, each time it breaks,
makes powdered bone and zinc for silverpoint.

And here, he deepens the black and so the density
of the light; light makes the edge, the line.
Yet it's not the line itself that gives us possibility,

but where the line is interrupted, veiled by fine
mist. And between black time and white eternity
he leaves us, at our north-most north imagining.

II

He leaves us at our north-most north imagining,
sails where currents pluck blistered wrack
through the Pillars of Hercules, where ships crack
and fling their silk on rock, where the sea sings

with Atlantic memory. Hear low whispering
as the wind whips waves into ribs, cloaks
muscled figures of the classical world, sucks
fish to the surface, throws them back as coins.

Here he shepherds the waves, makes light descend
in bones of rain, breaks a white wave on the fan
of a dark wave roaring free, lets souls ascend.

And now he spreads a shadow where the world ends
so we cannot know where God turns back and Man
begins, only borders the photographer intends.

III

Begins, ends, borders the photographer intends
for Africa, Cape Verde where the sea cries
in syncopated rhythm, where the sea sighs
and hisses 'what is – what is the sea' but veins

and wraiths and vortices? Here feel the dense
suck of a wave that curls and tucks, rises
and breathes, its arc muscular and fresh and high.
Watch its luminous haul lease height and length

to foam. He nearly died for this, stretched low
counting waves from low tide to high tide, his eye
abandoned to gold, to the promise of tone.

Awoke in hospital: tripod, camera by his pillow,
lens, black hoods, all exact, and knowing why
time itself gives east and west, above, below.

IV

Time itself gives east and west, above, below:
see Cap Manuel, basalt, schist, in Dakar night
where rock is charged, hand-placed by light,
each edge distinct, its surface hallowed.

And beyond the lit rock, a soundless mellow
sea where a single wave cast faintly left to right
divides the picture. The line creates angle, invites
measure: geometry on geology. A double arrow

carved white in black rock excites the reach –
Africa to America – human crossing, touch point.
Here we apprehend the language of *extreme*,

extremity, furthest from centre, to follow the sea's
milk thread, know the meaning of *front*
line: a breath begun at dawn in east-most east.

V

Line: the breath begun at dawn in east-most east
now declares immanence in merciless spray
that foams and flies through soaked rock drapes,
fires and dies at sea-snakes' throats, that feasts

itself on light. This is Robben Island, its coast
facing out to Cape Town on Freedom Day,
the photographer waiting in as the sea flays
all thought from mind, strips it of its violence.

The spray falls abstract into an inner frame,
and here he renders mass, allows light to speak
yet holds the light between lit fingers,

holds in tension dark and light, wild, tame,
to touch below the surface, beyond technique.
Even in the formless white, form lingers.

VI

Even in the formless white, form lingers.
In straws of silver rain; in time dropped frozen
from a moon-stained sky on the West Norwegian
Sea, where light fillets the waves and mirrored

air is a dress – lit clouds dress the water.
A white ball flashes and rises behind the rain
and floats, all surface, forsaking horizon:
light answering dark as the sea aligns its feathers.

Here he defies land: there is only sea and man,
and life in lengths he chooses. Here is Wilde's
optimism over experience, hope flung open,

concept sacrificed to lust: pure, raw, found
in the double image, the moon and its bride.
This, the photographer's point of no return.

VII

And this, the photographer's point of no return:
at the mouths of four rivers, at first light
or last, light buried beneath the water's sight
and named 'very light grey, grey', texture

a mask; and 'silver, very dark grey – almost
black'. The task, one single exposure, tide
measured, shadows suspended, pattern denied.
Comet Trail, Madeira; Bay of Biscay: never

chanced, each frame a double edge: end, start,
the sea's skim from Old World to mewling
New, only compass laying north and south apart –

and 'The sky very slightly burned in'. A chart
of the sea's inhuman gift of nothing or everything,
a record of a wave rising, falling, in a human heart.

BIOGRAPHICAL NOTES

ALICE ALLEN was born in London and grew up in Jersey in the Channel Islands. Her poems have been published in *The Rialto* and *Magma* and were commended in the 2005 New Writing Ventures poetry competition. She recently completed an M.Phil. in Writing at the University of Glamorgan.

LINDA BLACK studied Fine Art at Leeds and etching at the Slade School. She ran Apollo Etching Studio in London and has exhibited widely. Her poems appear in the anthology *Entering the Tapestry* (Enitharmon, 2003). She received the 2004/2005 Poetry School Scholorship and won the 2006 New Writing Ventures Award for poetry.

JEMMA BORG has a doctorate in genetics from Oxford. She has worked as a teacher overseas, an environmental researcher and a science editor. Her poems have appeared in magazines including *Magma*, *Poetry London*, *Scintilla* and the *Agenda* broadsheet for young poets. A selection is forthcoming in *Oxford Poets 2007* (Oxford Poets/Carcanet, 2007).

CAROLE BROMLEY is a teacher from York and a graduate of the M.Phil. in Writing at the University of Glamorgan. She was a first-stage winner of the 2004 Poetry Business Competition and read at The Aldeburgh Poetry Festival in 2005.

CLAIRE CROWTHER is studying for a Ph.D. in contemporary English poetry at Kingston University. She has had poems published in *Ambit*, *New Welsh Review*, *PN Review*, *Poetry Review*, *Poetry Wales* and the *TLS*, as well as in a pamphlet, *Glass Harmonica* (Flarestack, 2003).

PATRICK EARLY recently retired from an overseas career with the British Council, spending long periods in South America, the Balkans and the Arab World, often in places more violent and disturbing than glamorous (for example, in Yugoslavia under Milosevic). He has always written poetry, but since retirement has become a dedicated poet.

LUCY HAMILTON joined the Poetry School in 1998. Her poems have appeared in magazines and the anthologies *Parents* (Enitharmon/Second Light, 2000), *Making Worlds* (Headland, 2003), *In the Company of Poets* (Hearing Eye, 2003) and *Four Caves of the Heart* (Second Light, 2004). She teaches Chinese girls at a school in Kent.

LOUISA HOOPER is an editor of *Brittle Star* magazine and has been published in *Tabla*, *Magma* and *Citizen 32*. She graduated from Cambridge in English Literature and gained a Masters in Creative Writing at Bath Spa University. Having taught English in Japan and the UK, she now works in publishing in London.

VALERIE JOSEPHS studied Fine Art in London, Chicago and Glasgow. Her poems have been published in magazines and anthologies including *The Virago Book of Christmas* (2003), *Gobby Deegan's Riposte* (Donut Press, 2004) and in a pamphlet, *Green Minx* (Lizard's Leg Press, 2005). She was a prizewinner in the 2005 Yorkshire Poetry Competition.

JENNY LEWIS works regularly with actors, musicians and dancers, and teaches poetry at Oxford University. Her poetry has been performed at the Royal Festival Hall and published by Iron Press, Bilingua in Russia, and in *Oxford Poets 2000* (Oxford Poets/Carcanet, 2000). Her collection, *Fathom*, is forthcoming from Oxford Poets/Carcanet.

MARY MACRAE has studied with the Poetry School since October 1997. She has been published in a variety of magazines and the anthologies *Entering the Tapestry* (Enitharmon, 2003), *Making Worlds* (Headland, 2003) and *Four Caves of the Heart* (Second Light, 2004).

LORRAINE MARINER was born in Essex in 1974 and still lives in Upminster. Having read English at Huddersfield University and Library and Information Studies at University College, London, she currently works in the Tate Library and Archive at Tate Britain. She received an Arts Council England East writer's award in 2005.

BARBARA MARSH is an American who has lived in London since 1984. A musician/singer-songwriter, she is one half of The Dear Janes. Her work has appeared in, among other publications, *The Interpreter's House* and *Parents* (Enitharmon/Second Light, 2000). She recently completed an M.Phil. in Writing at the University of Glamorgan.

KAREN MCCARTHY's *The Worshipful Company of Pomegranate Slicers* (Spread the Word, 2006) was a *New Statesman* Book of the Year. She edited *Bittersweet: Contemporary Black Women's Poetry* (The Women's Press, 1998) and *Kin: New Fiction by Black and Asian Women* (Serpent's Tail, 2003) and is a contributing editor of the literary journal *Wasafiri*.

DAVID PENN was born in 1958 in Dartford, Kent. He writes both poetry and fiction, and has been published in *Magma*, *Smith's Knoll*, *Midnight Street* and *Urthona*, a Buddhist arts magazine. His work has also appeared in *The Heart as Origami* (Rising Fire Press, 2005), an anthology devoted to contemporary Buddhist poets.

DERRICK PORTER was born in London and grew up in Hoxton. He wrote his first poem aged thirteen and his second in his mid-twenties. He has two children and three grandchildren. His poems have been published in *Envoi*, *Magma*, *New Writer*, *Interpreter's House*, Poetry Library Web and in several competition anthologies.

SHAZEA QURAISHI was born in Pakistan, emigrated to Canada aged ten, and lived in Madrid before moving to London in 1994. As well as writing poetry, she has written a book for children and is working on a novel.

KATHRYN SIMMONDS was born in Hertfordshire in 1972 and now lives in north London. She received an Eric Gregory Award in 2002, won the 2006 Poetry London Competition, and her pamphlet, *Snug*, was a first-stage winner of the 2003 Poetry Business Competition. Her poems appear in the anthology *Seren Selections* (Seren, 2006).

SARADHA SOOBRAYEN received an Eric Gregory Award in 2004. She is the poetry editor of *Chroma: a queer literary journal*. Her fiction appears in *Kin: New Fiction by Black and Asian Women* (Serpent's Tail, 2003), her poems in *This Little Stretch of Life* (Hearing Eye, 2006) and *New Poetries IV* (Carcanet, 2007).

KAY SYRAD's poetry has appeared in journals and anthologies. She often collaborates with visual artists, and in 2000 received a Year of the Artist Award for *Making Work Visible*, a writing and photographic project in a sand-casting foundry. She works in education and is also a freelance writer and researcher.

ACKNOWLEDGEMENTS

Alice Allen: 'The Sea's Loan to the City' appeared on the 2005 New Writing Ventures website.

Jemma Borg: 'As Flamingos at the Water's Edge' (under the title 'Burglary') in *Agenda* broadsheets for young poets, number 1 (2003); 'The Mathematician' was a runner-up in *Mslexia*'s Women's Poetry Competition 2004; 'How It Is with the Circle' in *Oxford Magazine*; 'Do I Still Think of You?' in *Asia Literary Review*.

Carole Bromley: 'The Homecoming of Sir Thomas Wyatt' won the Yorkshire Prize 2000; 'The Last Time' in *Anon*; 'Away' won a prize in the New Forest Poetry Society Competition 2002. All three poems are included in *Unscheduled Halt* (Smith/Doorstop, 2005).

Claire Crowther: 'Untitled' in *The Times Literary Supplement*; 'Nudists' in *Poetry Review*; 'The Wyvern' and 'Empire' in *Poetry Wales*.

Patrick Early: 'The Windharp' in *Magma*; 'The Burning of the Maps' in *The Burning Bush*.

Valerie Josephs: 'Correspondence' in *Magma*; 'Dry' in *Green Minx* (Lizard's Leg Press, 2005).

Jenny Lewis: 'Woman Brushing Her Hair' won a New Writers Prize in 1997 and was included in *Oxford Poets 2000* (Oxford Poets/Carcanet, 2000).

Mary MacRae: 'Glose' in *PN Review* and *Images of Women* (Second Light/ Arrowhead Press, 2006); 'Gannet' in *London Poets 2*; 'The Clearing' in *Scintilla*.

Lorraine Mariner: 'My Beast' in *Magma*; 'Lieserl Einstein' in *Magma* and *A decade of difference: Magma Poetry's tenth anniversary anthology*; 'Mac' in *The Rialto*. All four poems are included in *Bye for now* (The Rialto, 2005).

Karen McCarthy's 'The Worshipful Company of Pomegranate Slicers' is included in a chapbook of the same title (Spread the Word, 2006).

David Penn: 'A Woman Observed in a Pub' in *Magma*; all three poems are included in *The Heart as Origami* (Rising Fire Press, 2005).

Derrick Porter: 'After the Storm' won second prize in the Ripley Poetry Association Open Competition; 'The Carriers' in *Envoi*.

Shazea Quraishi: 'Skyros' (under the title 'Found') in *Magma*; 'Still Light' in *The Interpreter's House* and *Images of Women* (Second Light/Arrowhead Press, 2006); 'All This Time' in *Smiths Knoll*.

Kathryn Simmonds: 'Leftovers' in *Poetry London*; 'The Dead Are Dead' in *PN Review*.

Saradha Soobrayen: 'Like Cold Air Passing through Lips', 'On the Water Meadows', 'Questioning the Invisible Stitching' and 'My Conqueror' in *Wasafari*.